An Analysis of

Thomas Kuhn's

The Structure of Scientific Revolutions

Jo Hedesan
with
Joseph Tendler

Published by Macat International Ltd
24:13 Coda Centre, 189 Munster Road, London SW6 6AW.

Distributed exclusively by Routledge
2 Park Square, Milton Park, Abingdon, Oxon OX14 4RN
711 Third Avenue, New York, NY 10017, USA

Routledge is an imprint of the Taylor & Francis Group, an informa business

www.macat.com
info@macat.com

Cataloguing in Publication Data
A catalogue record for this book is available from the British Library.
Library of Congress Cataloguing-in-Publication Data is available upon request.
Cover illustration: Etienne Gilfillan

ISBN 978-1-912302-70-3 (hardback)
ISBN 978-1-912127-85-6 (paperback)
ISBN 978-1-912281-58-9 (e-book)

Notice

CONTENTS

THE MACAT LIBRARY

The Macat Library is a series of unique academic explorations of seminal works in the humanities and social sciences – books and papers that have had a significant and widely recognised impact on their disciplines. It has been created to serve as much more than just a summary of what lies between the covers of a great book. It illuminates and explores the influences on, ideas of, and impact of that book. Our goal is to offer a learning resource that encourages critical thinking and fosters a better, deeper understanding of important ideas.

Each publication is divided into three Sections: Influences, Ideas, and Impact. Each Section has four Modules. These explore every important facet of the work, and the responses to it.

This Section-Module structure makes a Macat Library book easy to use, but it has another important feature. Because each Macat book is written to the same format, it is possible (and encouraged!) to cross-reference multiple Macat books along the same lines of inquiry or research. This allows the reader to open up interesting interdisciplinary pathways.

To further aid your reading, lists of glossary terms and people mentioned are included at the end of this book (these are indicated by an asterisk [*] throughout) – as well as a list of works cited.

Macat has worked with the University of Cambridge to identify the elements of critical thinking and understand the ways in which six different skills combine to enable effective thinking.
Three allow us to fully understand a problem; three more give us the tools to solve it. Together, these six skills make up the **PACIER** model of critical thinking. They are:

ANALYSIS – understanding how an argument is built
EVALUATION – exploring the strengths and weaknesses of an argument
INTERPRETATION – understanding issues of meaning

CREATIVE THINKING – coming up with new ideas and fresh connections
PROBLEM-SOLVING – producing strong solutions
REASONING – creating strong arguments

To find out more, visit **WWW.MACAT.COM.**

CRITICAL THINKING AND *THE STRUCTURE OF SCIENTIFIC REVOLUTIONS*

Primary critical thinking skill: CREATIVE THINKING
Secondary critical thinking skill: REASONING

Thomas Kuhn's *The Structure of Scientific Revolutions* can be seen, without exaggeration, as a landmark text in intellectual history.

In his analysis of shifts in scientific thinking, Kuhn questioned the prevailing view that science was an unbroken progression towards the truth. Progress was actually made, he argued, via "paradigm shifts", meaning that evidence that existing scientific models are flawed slowly accumulates – in the face, at first, of opposition and doubt – until it finally results in a crisis that forces the development of a new model. This development, in turn, produces a period of rapid change – "extraordinary science," Kuhn terms it – before an eventual return to "normal science" begins the process whereby the whole cycle eventually repeats itself.

This portrayal of science as the product of successive revolutions was the product of rigorous but imaginative critical thinking. It was at odds with science's self-image as a set of disciplines that constantly evolve and progress via the process of building on existing knowledge. Kuhn's highly creative re-imagining of that image has proved enduringly influential – and is the direct product of the author's ability to produce a novel explanation for existing evidence and to redefine issues so as to see them in new ways.

ABOUT THE AUTHOR OF THE ORIGINAL WORK

Born in Cincinnati, Ohio, in 1922, **Thomas Kuhn** knew by the age of 18 that he wanted to be a scientist. He studied physics at Harvard University, obtaining his PhD there after a break with academia to serve in the military during World War II. Three years as a Junior Harvard Fellow then gave Kuhn academic freedom, and he took full advantage by moving towards history and the philosophy of science – areas where he would go on to make his mark. Kuhn died in 1996, having both challenged his academic colleagues and changed the way the general public thinks about an entire range of disciplines.

ABOUT THE AUTHORS OF THE ANALYSIS

Dr Jo Hedesan lectures at Oxford and is a Wellcome Trust Research Fellow in Medical History and Humanities at the university.

Dr Joseph Tendler received his PhD from the University of St Andrews. He is a specialist in historiography, the study of how history is conceived and written, and is the author of *Opponents of the Annales School*.

ABOUT MACAT

GREAT WORKS FOR CRITICAL THINKING

Macat is focused on making the ideas of the world's great thinkers accessible and comprehensible to everybody, everywhere, in ways that promote the development of enhanced critical thinking skills.

It works with leading academics from the world's top universities to produce new analyses that focus on the ideas and the impact of the most influential works ever written across a wide variety of academic disciplines. Each of the works that sit at the heart of its growing library is an enduring example of great thinking. But by setting them in context – and looking at the influences that shaped their authors, as well as the responses they provoked – Macat encourages readers to look at these classics and game-changers with fresh eyes. Readers learn to think, engage and challenge their ideas, rather than simply accepting them.

'Macat offers an amazing first-of-its-kind tool for interdisciplinary learning and research. Its focus on works that transformed their disciplines and its rigorous approach, drawing on the world's leading experts and educational institutions, opens up a world-class education to anyone.'

Andreas Schleicher
Director for Education and Skills, Organisation for Economic
Co-operation and Development

'Macat is taking on some of the major challenges in university education ... They have drawn together a strong team of active academics who are producing teaching materials that are novel in the breadth of their approach.'

Prof Lord Broers,
former Vice-Chancellor of the University of Cambridge

'The Macat vision is exceptionally exciting. It focuses upon new modes of learning which analyse and explain seminal texts which have profoundly influenced world thinking and so social and economic development. It promotes the kind of critical thinking which is essential for any society and economy. This is the learning of the future.'

Rt Hon Charles Clarke, former UK Secretary of State for Education

'The Macat analyses provide immediate access to the critical conversation surrounding the books that have shaped their respective discipline, which will make them an invaluable resource to all of those, students and teachers, working in the field.'

Professor William Tronzo, University of California at San Diego

WAYS IN TO THE TEXT

KEY POINTS

- Thomas Samuel Kuhn (1922–96) was an American physicist, historian, and philosopher of science.

- In *The Structure of Scientific Revolutions* (1962) he argued that all advances in scientific knowledge resulted from "revolutions" in scientific knowledge.

- The book transformed the notion of science and the way in which science develops as a practice shaped by scientists and their methods.

Who Was Thomas Kuhn?

Thomas Kuhn was born in 1922 in Cincinnati, Ohio. His parents were Samuel L. Kuhn, an industrial engineer, and Minette Stroock Kuhn, whom he would later describe as "the intellectual in the family." [1] He published *The Structure of Scientific Revolutions* in 1962, when he was 40 years old.

By the time Kuhn graduated from high school, he knew that he wanted to pursue mathematics and physics. After attending boarding school on the east coast of the United States, he enrolled at Harvard University* in 1940. Once he had received his undergraduate degree, he spent two years in the military working on radar technology.

America's decision to deploy atomic bombs in 1945 near the end of World War II,* destroying two Japanese cities, reminded the world that science's power to shape human destiny was an awesome responsibility. Kuhn decided to address this by going beyond the applications of science to study the principles underlying science itself.

After the war, Kuhn resumed academic study and in 1949 gained his PhD from Harvard, where the university's president, the scientist James Bryant Conant,* became his mentor. Conant, who had helped develop the atomic bomb, enlisted many renowned scholars in an effort to enhance the popularity of science. Thomas Kuhn, then unknown, was one of them.

Largely because of Conant's influence, Kuhn made teaching the history and philosophy of science* his areas of expertise. Before Kuhn published *The Structure of Scientific Revolutions*, the history of science* was seen as a sideline—interesting, but not worthy material for an academic discipline. Kuhn's work changed that. It also brought a number of scientific concepts into the mainstream, including "paradigm"* (roughly, a model of knowledge that explains the results of scientific experiments), "scientific revolution"* (the moment one paradigm gives way to another), and "paradigm shift"* (the intellectual and scientific consequences of a scientific revolution).

What Does *The Structure of Scientific Revolutions* Say?

Scientists had always seen their work as linear, with each new advance adding to and enhancing the store of scientific knowledge amassed since ancient times. In *The Structure of Scientific Revolutions*, however, Thomas Kuhn argued that science was cyclical. That is, progress occurs in repeating phases.

As Kuhn saw it, a period of "normal science"* would end when scientists overturned the prevailing paradigm, creating a period of "revolutionary science."* Rather than building on established stores of knowledge, the breakthroughs made in this revolutionary period permanently change the way scientists understand the world. In addition to the concepts of "paradigm" and "revolutionary science," Kuhn introduced a third concept: "incommensurability."*

Scientists overturning a prevailing paradigm are required to replace it. The new paradigm, offering a different and sometimes opposing account of reality, will be "incommensurable"—that is, the two paradigms have no common or shared means of explaining reality. So the selection of a "consensus paradigm"* at the end of a scientific revolution is as much a matter of choice by scientists as it is based on the power of the paradigm to explain reality.

If scientists in any given era see the world in the same way, Kuhn claims, it is because they use the same paradigm. But that does not mean the world is exactly as they observe it. The world's reality exists independently of the observer. When the paradigm changes, it is not the *world* that changes but the *scientist*, who now observes the world from a different perspective. This is a point some readers of Kuhn have failed to grasp, believing instead that he meant "paradigm shift" to refer to a world-altering event.

Kuhn turns to history to validate his theory. In the eighteenth century, the French chemist Antoine Lavoisier* discovered oxygen. Oxygen pre-existed this discovery, of course; humans had been breathing it for a very long time before Lavoisier's birth. Lavoisier's discovery, Kuhn explains, changed the paradigm. The world had not changed. But scientists never saw it in the same way again.

The Structure of Scientific Revolutions retains a wide readership more than 50 years after its initial publication. By 2003, the work had sold over a million copies and been translated into at least 20 different languages. *Structure* has indeed changed the way scientists look at their endeavors. Although some disagree with Kuhn's conclusions—indeed, one long-running disagreement was labeled "the science wars"*— *Structure* attracted readers inside and outside of science because it captured a spirit of questioning that seemed to pervade society in the early 1960s. There was a "paradigm shift" in the air, it seemed. So Kuhn's work about shifting ideas in science fitted perfectly with wider discussions taking place.

The academic discipline of sociology* (the study of the structure and history of human societies) grew more popular during this period. Sociologists had always looked at how social conditions shaped ideas; now they studied how social conditions had shaped science and historians of science.

The general public was also highly attuned to science during this period. Many, such as Kuhn's mentor James Bryant Conant, saw science as key to winning the tense standoff of the Cold War* between the United States and the Soviet Union.* But increasing numbers of people struggled to reconcile that goal with the potential devastation of a nuclear war. People questioned the role that scientists played in developing such destructive weapons.

Structure served as a springboard for these ideas. Some of the conclusions people drew from the work surprised Kuhn. A few even worried him. He had, after all, been writing about the internal structure of science, not about the power of ideas to change the world. But there was no doubt that Kuhn's work opened the door to questioning. And that door will likely not close again.

Why Does *The Structure of Scientific Revolutions* Matter?

Thomas Kuhn's idea of "revolutionary" periods of science upended centuries of established wisdom. Before Kuhn, scientists believed that they were detached observers, building upon the objective observations and discoveries of the scientists who had come before. After Kuhn published *The Structure of Scientific Revolutions*, those comforting certainties no longer applied.

In that sense, *Structure* is itself revolutionary. It changed the way people look at the world around them—so much so that "paradigm" and "paradigm shift" have entered general usage. Although Kuhn intended the term "paradigm" to apply to science, scholars have imported it into other academic disciplines. The world of commerce has adopted it, too. Unsurprisingly, "paradigm" now appears on lists of words that have been so overused as to become meaningless.

Although Kuhn intended the book to influence readers interested in the history and philosophy of science, it has also influenced scientists in other fields, teachers of science, academics interested in the sociology of science, and even the general public. Today, radical intellectuals remain attuned to Kuhn's ideas. *Structure* has become a foundational text for people interested in postmodernist* critiques of science. Roughly, these approaches, often employing the theory that science is simply another culturally bound method of producing narratives, are frequently used to demonstrate ways in which historically marginalized groups such as women, people of color, and colonial subjects, have impacted on the development of science. The new discipline of the sociology of scientific knowledge,* meanwhile, maintains that social conditions affect the creation of scientific knowledge—a very Kuhnian view.

While many scientists continue to disagree with Kuhn, they acknowledge the large contribution his work made to science. One of his longstanding critics, the German American philosopher of science Carl Hempel,* acknowledged as much. Paying tribute to Kuhn in 1993, Hempel wrote: "Whatever position your colleagues may take, Tom, I am sure that they all feel a large debt of gratitude to you for your provocative and illuminating ideas."[2]

Over half a century after its publication, *Structure* continues to inspire and provoke readers. Even scholars working in non-scientific fields speak of the "structure of revolutions" as Kuhn defined the term.

NOTES

1   N. M. Swerdlow, "Thomas S. Kuhn, A Biographical Memoir," *National Academy of Science*, (2013), accessed June 29, 2015, http://www.nasonline.org/publications/biographical-memoirs/memoir-pdfs/kuhn-thomas.pdf

2   Carl Hempel, "Thomas Kuhn: Colleague and Friend," in *World Changes: Thomas Kuhn and the Nature of Science*, ed. Paul Horwich (Cambridge, MA: MIT Press, 1003), 7–8.

SECTION 1
INFLUENCES

THE AUTHOR AND THE HISTORICAL CONTEXT

KEY POINTS

- *The Structure of Scientific Revolutions* presents an ongoing challenge to the notion that science can discover the truth about what reality "is."

- Thomas Kuhn's work as a radar technologist and his graduate studies in physics left him dissatisfied with fundamental aspects of how scholars and the public understood science.

- Kuhn's work was shaped by the events of World War II* and the Cold War* (a long period of frequently grave political tension between the United States and its allies and the Soviet Union* and its allies).

Why Read This Text?

Thomas Kuhn's *The Structure of Scientific Revolutions* presents a thorough analysis of how scientific knowledge evolves. Regularly found on lists of "best books of the twentieth century," and one of the most popular non-fiction books of the last half-century, Kuhn's work changed the way scientists approached their task and the way we think about breakthroughs, whether in science or in other spheres of human endeavor. Its key concepts—"paradigm,"* an intellectual model for understanding the world; "scientific revolution,"* the moment when one paradigm gives way to another; and "paradigm shift,"* the state of affairs after a scientific revolution—have entered the popular vocabulary.

Although the idea that changes in human understanding can be revolutionary has entered everyday language,[1] the work's core

> ❝ A softer skepticism, one more sympathetic to the aspirations of science, does not renounce the possibility of objective truth, but instead is agnostic about that possibility. Thomas Kuhn is such a skeptic. ❞
>
> Mike W. Martin, *Creativity: Ethics and Excellence in Science*

question—what forces can change the ways scientists think and work?—remains hotly debated today. Previously, the idea of a scientific revolution had been narrowly applied to physics. Kuhn extended the term to apply to all areas of science; his many readers have used it to refer to intellectual endeavor in general.[2]

Kuhn's notion of science as a constantly evolving body of knowledge has affected political culture, both in his native United States and throughout the West. His conclusions demonstrate the provisional and uncertain nature of scientific knowledge, while his historical analysis of the evolution of science gave rise to the discipline of the history of science*; this showed that scientific knowledge, rather than being fixed and certain, actually changed over time.[3]

If science is provisional rather than definitive, however, politicians and public figures can no longer hold up scientific findings as absolute proof of anything.[4]

Author's Life

Kuhn was a scientist for much of his life. At school he developed a love for mathematics and physics[5] and went on to Harvard University,* completing his undergraduate and doctoral studies in physics by 1949.[6] Harvard's influential president James Bryant Conant* helped Kuhn obtain professional positions in the history and science departments.[7]

Conant had been an important figure in the development of science during World War II. As administrator of the research and development program known as the Manhattan Project,* he not only helped develop the atomic bomb but convinced US President Harry S.Truman* that its use was inevitable.[8] After the war, Conant returned to the presidency of Harvard and began a project to bring science to a wider audience—both in academia and in the public. He enlisted the support of such senior scholars as the Belgian émigré historian of science and chemist George Sarton* as well as junior scholars such as Kuhn.[9]

In the course of his career Kuhn continued Conant's undertaking, devoting himself to teaching the history and philosophy of science* in ways accessible to both the general public and scholars. In 1961, he became a professor of the history of science at the University of California,* where he wrote *The Structure of Scientific Revolutions.* On leaving in 1964, Kuhn taught at Princeton University* and the equally prestigious Massachusetts Institute of Technology.* He also served for a year as president of the History of Science Society.*[10]

Before the 1960s—that is to say, before the publication of *The Structure of Scientific Revolutions*—scientists who wished to write about the history of science did so as a sideline to their main jobs.[11] Kuhn's work changed that. He made it possible for scientists to cross over from physics to the history and philosophy of science. In doing so, he changed the world's understanding of science forever.

Author's Background

After receiving his undergraduate degree from Harvard during World War II, Kuhn spent two years in the military working on radar technology. His occupation left him unhappy with how the world outside of academia applied and practiced science. After the war he returned to Harvard for postgraduate study.[12] Although formally a student of physics, he also wanted to look beyond the application of science in the world to the underlying principles of scientific knowledge itself.[13]

In 1945, near the end of World War II, the American government forced Japan's surrender by unleashing a display of overwhelming military force—the detonation of the atomic bomb, which Kuhn's mentor, Conant, had helped to develop. The bomb destroyed two Japanese cities, Hiroshima* and Nagasaki,* and prompted politicians and the general public to ask whether it was morally justifiable to use science and technology in warfare.[14] Whatever view people took, events seized public attention: scientific discoveries had the power to shape human destiny.

The Cold War, which began as World War II ended and lasted until around 1991, also shaped Kuhn's views about science. America's rivalry with the Soviet Union saw scientific and technological progress became topics of public debate; in particular, Kuhn focused on the development of nuclear weapons, and the threat that nuclear war could break out between these two powerful nations. Physics played a central role in these major developments. The Canadian historian of science Ian Hacking* writes that during this time, "everybody knew that physics was where the action was"[15]—including Kuhn. The science of physics and its foundational principles and characteristics were ripe for analysis. Kuhn's whole career can be seen as a response to this challenge.

NOTES

1   Thomas Nickles, "Introduction," in *Thomas Kuhn*, ed. Thomas Nickles (Cambridge: Cambridge University Press, 2003), 1; Ian Hacking, "Introductory Essay," in Thomas S. Kuhn, *The Structure of Scientific Revolutions*, 4th ed. (Chicago, IL: University of Chicago Press, 2012), xxxvii.

2   Kuhn, *Structure*, 32.

3   Christopher Green, "Where Is Kuhn Going?," *American Psychologist* 59, no. 4 (2004): 271–2.

4   Ian Hacking, *The Social Construction of What?* (Cambridge, MA: Harvard University Press, 1999), 12.

5   Alexander Bird, "Thomas Kuhn," *The Stanford Encyclopedia of Philosophy* (Winter 2014 Edition), Edward N. Zalta, ed., http://plato.stanford.edu/archives/win2012/entries/davidson/>.

6   Bird, "Thomas Kuhn."

7   Steve Fuller, *Thomas Kuhn: A Philosophical History for Our Times* (Chicago, IL: University of Chicago Press, 2000), 9–11.

8   Ziauddin Sardar, "Thomas Kuhn and the Science Wars," in *Postmodernism and Big Science*, ed. Richard Appignanesi (Cambridge: Icon Books, 2002), 200.

9   Fuller, *Thomas Kuhn*, 9–11.

10 Bird, "Thomas Kuhn."

11 Jeff Hughes, "Whigs, Prigs and Politics: Problems in the Historiography of Contemporary Science," in *The Historiography of Contemporary Science and Technology*, ed. Thomas Söderqvist (Amsterdam: Harwood Academic Publishers, 1997), 20–1.

12 Bird, "Thomas Kuhn."

13 Marnie Hughes-Warrington, "Thomas Samuel Kuhn," in *Fifty Key Thinkers in History* (London: Routledge, 2003), 188.

14 Thomas C. Reeves, *Twentieth-Century America: A Brief History* (Oxford: Oxford University Press, 2000), 137.

15 Hacking, "Introductory Essay," in Kuhn, *Structure*, ix.

ACADEMIC CONTEXT

KEY POINTS

- The fields of the history of science* and the philosophy of science* explain the evolving ways in which scientists have arrived at their conclusions.

- In the 1960s, scholars challenged the idea that science provides concrete, accurate results. Supporters of scientific realism* (who argue that a scientist's opinions do not necessarily affect their conclusions) faced off against supporters of scientific constructivism* (who argue that a scientist does not study reality directly—only information collected through experiments).

- Thomas Kuhn led the way in using historical analysis to undermine both logical empiricism* and logical positivism*—approaches to science and philosophy grounded in verifiability,* logic, and rationalism.*

The Work in its Context

Thomas Kuhn's work *The Structure of Scientific Revolutions* falls within the field of the history of science: the study of how scientific knowledge evolves over time, a field pioneered by leading sixteenth-century scientists such as Francis Bacon* in England and Johannes Kepler* in Germany. In their lifetimes, scientists such as Isaac Newton* (a physicist who outlined principles that continue to inform the study of physics today[1]) made significant discoveries. Bacon and Kepler wanted their histories of science to reconstruct a "usable past" showing how the "modern science" of their lifetimes had developed since earlier, "ancient wisdom."[2]

> ❝ Kuhn addressed philosophical questions about reason
> and evidence via an examination of history ... The
> logical empiricists made a sharp distinction between
> questions about the history and psychology of science,
> on the one hand, and questions about evidence and
> justification, on the other. Kuhn was deliberately mixing
> together things that logical empiricists had insisted
> should be kept apart. ❞
>
> Peter Godfrey-Smith, *Theory and Reality: An Introduction to the Philosophy
> of Science*

At the outset of the twentieth century, the history of science
remained little changed from Bacon and Kepler's day. Twentieth-
century historians of science, for instance, saw scientific knowledge as
an accumulation of facts and data. As scientific experiments added to
this store of facts, they saw science as having a linear trajectory, with all
new scientific discoveries building on previous discoveries to produce
"progress" in scientific knowledge. In addition, scientists passively
observed and recorded their results without injecting their own
opinions or prejudices into their findings.[3]

Overview of the Field

By the time Kuhn wrote *Structure* in 1962, the history of science had
witnessed significant, transformative developments. Previously it had
been written by scientists but now historians, even those without
formal scientific training, had become interested in the subject as
well.[4] The Belgian-born American scientist and historian George
Sarton* did the most to initiate this transition, explaining that
"historians of science must know history *and* science ... good
intentions are never enough."[5]

Historians studying science drew on an emerging historical sub-discipline: the history of ideas.* Pioneered in the US by the German-born American philosopher and historian Arthur O. Lovejoy,* the history of ideas showed how ideas evolved to mean different things over the centuries. Lovejoy "diligently developed the discipline, framing it as a study of purely cognitive worldviews* and their component 'unit ideas'."*6

In other words, Lovejoy argued that people, scientists included, respond to the world by forming mental images—"cognitive worldviews." They use these mental images to connect the collection of ideas they hold in their minds, isolated ideas he called "unit ideas." Any idea about the world, whether of science, gravity or death, for example, would change over time because people would put their unit ideas together in different ways. So, different people, places, and eras would hold different ideas about science, gravity or death—or anything else they constructed from their unit ideas.

Academic Influences

Kuhn's influences came from scholars working in science, in social science, and in the history of science. He also benefited from interactions between these disciplines.

When the scientist and Harvard University president James Bryant Conant* set out to educate the public about science, he enlisted Kuhn's help. In researching public science education, Kuhn noticed a contrast between "modern science" and the "ancient wisdom" Kepler and Bacon had written about.[7] Conant also introduced Kuhn to Sarton—another member of the science education program—and learned about Sarton's innovative ways of thinking about the history of science.[8]

Scholars from the social sciences, psychology, and linguistics inspired Kuhn to think in new ways about how people's minds and language shape the way they see the world.

The French psychologist Jean Piaget's* theories of child development and the experiments of the school of Gestalt psychology* both emphasized that people use a theoretical framework to analyze the world around them. Kuhn accepted this.[9] In other words, he agreed that our thought processes could not be separated from what we know about the world. From linguistics, Kuhn learned about the ways context changes the meaning of words. This reinforced his understanding of Piaget's psychology that each individual had different perspectives.

Kuhn's greatest influence, however, was the Austrian-British philosopher Ludwig Wittgenstein.* Wittgenstein argued that when individuals say something about the world, they are "interpreting," and "when we interpret we form hypotheses, which may prove false."[10] In other words, people may see the world incorrectly even though what they say is true at any given moment.

Wittgenstein was inspired to write his theory of language by the eighteenth-century German philosopher Immanuel Kant.* Kuhn also studied him closely. Kant identified four categories one could use to analyze anything: quantity, quality, relation, and modality. Using these categories, Kant could describe an object in terms both of its own characteristics and by reference to the context in which it existed. Previous philosophers had focused on just one or the other.[11] In other words, Kant's categories allowed him to formulate a way of interpreting how physical objects would behave.

Kuhn also wanted to explain scientific activity with reference to foundational concepts. Kant's categories informed Wittgenstein's twentieth-century theory of how we use language to interpret the world. By extension, Kant's ideas showed Kuhn how our everyday speech shaped our understanding of the world.

Historians of science inspired Kuhn to focus on the role cultural assumptions play in scientific conclusions. Alexandre Koyré,* a French Russian scholar who immigrated to America, resurrected the idea that scientific knowledge progressed because of changes, or revolutions, in the way scientists thought.[12] Kuhn also found thought-provoking the French philosopher of science Hélène Metzger's* work on seventeenth-century chemistry and the German historian Anneliese Maier's* work on medieval science. But maybe the most important source of inspiration to Kuhn was the work on tacit knowledge* (roughly, the kind of knowledge not easily transferred from one person to another by the simple act of writing or speaking) of Hungarian British scholar Michael Polanyi,* who excelled in many disciplines. Polanyi's thinking encouraged Kuhn to investigate the ways in which cultural attitudes, as much as scientific method, shaped and could be detected in scientists' conclusions.[13]

NOTES

1   A. Rupert Hall, *The Revolution in Science 1500–1750* (London: Longman, 1983), 134, 143.

2   Hall, *Revolution in Science 1500–1750*, 18.

3   Thomas S. Kuhn, *The Structure of Scientific Revolutions*, 4th ed. (Chicago, IL: University of Chicago Press, 2012), 31.

4   Jeff Hughes, "Whigs, Prigs and Politics: Problems in the Historiography of Contemporary Science," in *The Historiography of Contemporary Science and Technology*, ed. Thomas Söderqvist (Amsterdam: Harwood Academic Publishers, 1997), 20.

5   George Sarton, *A Guide to the History of Science* (Waltham, MA: Chronica Botanica Co, 1952), ix–x.

6   Andrew Jewett, *Science, Democracy and the American University: From the Civil War to the Cold War* (Cambridge: University of Cambridge Press, 2012), 257.

7   Thomas Kuhn, *The Road Since Structure: Philosophical Essays, 1970–1993 with an Autobiographical Interview*, ed. James Conant and John Haugeland (Chicago, IL: Chicago University Press, 2000), 16.

8   Steve Fuller, *Thomas Kuhn: A Philosophical History for Our Times* (Chicago, IL: University of Chicago Press, 2000), 9–11.

9   Kuhn, *The Structure of Scientific Revolutions*, "Preface," xi.

10   Ludwig Wittgenstein, *Philosophical Investigations*, 3rd ed. (Oxford: Blackwell, 2003), 181.

11   Michela Massimi, "Philosophy and the Sciences After Kant," in *Conceptions of Philosophy*, ed. Anthony O'Hear (Cambridge: Cambridge University Press, 2000), 282.

12   Paul Hoyningen-Huene, *Reconstructing Scientific Revolutions: Thomas S. Kuhn's Philosophy of Science* (Chicago, IL: University of Chicago Press, 1993), xix.

13   Alexander Bird, *Thomas Kuhn* (Chesham: Acumen, 2000), 14–20.

MODULE 3
THE PROBLEM

KEY POINTS

- Historians of science question whether scientists work objectively, studying reality unaffected by their personal views or professional positions.

- Logical empiricists* argue that scientists verify all their discoveries by reference to scientific data. But historians of science contend that the concept of evidence itself has changed over time, making verification relative.

- Kuhn combines these positions, using verification and relativity to produce a new understanding of scientific knowledge.

Core Question

In *The Structure of Scientific Revolutions*, Thomas Kuhn sought "to clarify and deepen an understanding of *contemporary* scientific methods or concepts displaying their evolution."[1] In other words, he reframed the central question asked by historians of science since the discipline emerged in the sixteenth century: how do scientists find out about the real world?

This central question breaks down into two sets of questions: those about *scientists* and those about the *nature of reality itself*. Historians asked if scientists could escape their personal and cultural prejudices when they evaluated data. And they asked if reality exists independently of the mind of the scientist responsible for evaluating it.

These questions uncover a foundational problem that continues to divide historians and scientists.[2] On one side, "realists"* argue that scientists have direct access to the real world of objects and matter, and

> 66 There is an increasing tendency, now, to construe knowledge as a construct of historical experience and to challenge any principled disjunction between objectivity in natural sciences and in the human sciences and practical life. To favor these themes is, effectively, to deny any privilege or hierarchical order of knowledge favoring the natural sciences. 99
>
> Joseph Margolis, "Objectivity as a Problem"

that they analyze, experiment on and describe it. In this way, realists believe that scientists can uncover the truth without allowing their personal opinions to interfere with their research.[3] The world is as it is and it is plain for all scientists to see for themselves. Other scholars— "constructivists"*—hold the opposite view. They believe that scientists construct their own picture of reality. Scientists cannot help allowing their own ideas, perceptions, and intuitions to shape that picture. And their own research and their standing in the scientific community,* along with a host of intellectual and social variables, also shape their ideas of reality.[4]

The Participants

Before Kuhn published *The Structure of Scientific Revolutions*, realist and constructivist positions had their own representatives. Historians of science stood with the constructivists, and logical positivists or empiricists* (whose approach "is often summarized by saying that the only source of knowledge is experience")took the realist position.[5]

Before 1960, logical empiricism—a school in the philosophy of science* with roots in a tradition begun by the seventeenth-century English philosopher John Locke* and continued by the likes of the Scottish philosopher David Hume* in the eighteenth century and the German philosopher Ernst Mach* in the nineteenth—seemed the stronger argument. Around the time of World War I,* the German philosophers Rudolf Carnap,* Otto Neurath,* and Carl Hempel* perceived a decline in standards of philosophy. Their work—which came to be known as logical empiricism—served as a response to this.[6] Logical empiricism updated the classical empiricist tradition founded by Locke by adding two central ideas: the analytic–synthetic distinction,* and the idea of the verifiability theory of meaning.*

The German philosopher Immanuel Kant* introduced the idea of analytic–synthetic distinction in the seventeenth century. An analytic proposition* would be a statement such as "all bachelors are unmarried." The definition of a bachelor—an unmarried man—is contained in the proposition itself. By contrast, a synthetic proposition,* such as "all bachelors are unhappy," does not contain its definition. "Unhappy" is not part of the definition of "bachelor" and the statement may be true for some bachelors, but not for others. Logical empiricists paired this centuries-old concept with a newer one—the verificationist principle* which maintained that only two kinds of statements hold any real meaning: those that are logically necessary and those that can be verified by experiment. According to the idea of verification, another scientist can test what the first scientist comes to understand about the whole only by repeating her experiments, ensuring the validity of her analysis and synthesis.[7]

Combining analytic–synthetic distinction and the verifiability theory, logical empiricists would say that a scientist reaches an understanding of the *whole* perceived from experience of the world by using the rational process of analyzing and thinking about data relating to *parts of that whole*.[8]

Logical empiricists held that these basic concepts applied to all science at any time, and, as a result, that science continually accumulated new knowledge and discoveries as it had for the sixteenth-century originators of the history of science*: the English philosopher Francis Bacon* and the German astronomer Johannes Kepler.*

Historians, by contrast, occupied a constructivist position. As they saw it, scientists operated according to principles unique to their own age. Looking across the centuries, they saw science developing in an irregular, unpredictable manner. They insisted that to recreate an accurate history of science, one needed to "contextualize" scientific activity.

In the mid-twentieth century, historians of science pointed to the work of the late nineteenth-century French philosopher and historian Pierre Duhem* who argued that scholars need a "rationally reconstructed [history of science in which] only what was philosophically relevant was included."[9] Historians, in other words, should look at what scientists believed and how they acted on it. Historians of science should investigate this if they wanted to find out how science had evolved over time, instead of trying to apply general philosophical concepts as logical empiricists did.

The Contemporary Debate

By the 1960s, when Kuhn wrote *The Structure of Scientific Revolutions*, this debate between logical empiricists and historians had become entrenched. Overlaps developed between the two sides, and Kuhn took elements from each.

Both sides relied on a particular understanding of the role of language in creating knowledge. The logical empiricists had derived their theory of verifiability and the distinction between analysis and synthesis from the work of linguists. In addition to Kant, they drew on the philosophy of the twentieth-century philosopher Ludwig Wittgenstein,* both of whom, working centuries apart, emphasized underlying mental operations as key to understanding how individuals acquire knowledge.[10] Kuhn's interest in Kant confirmed his connection to the logical positivists; all wanted to ground their universal understanding of science on basic principles with logical foundations.[11]

Although Kuhn seldom associated himself publicly with the logical empiricists, he did associate himself with the contextual interpretation of science offered by constructivists. Indeed, he maintained that he conceived of *The Structure of Scientific Revolutions* as a stand against the logical empiricism that dominated science textbooks of the 1950s.[12] He claimed he did so by proposing that science operated in disjointed cycles—so scientific knowledge developed unevenly, an idea that stood in stark contrast to assumptions of the logical empiricists. He called his view a "historiographic revolution in the study of science" that borrowed extensively from Duhem, Alexandre Koyré* and others to promote a historical rather than a philosophical understanding of science.[13]

The history of science that emerged from the work of Duhem and the Franco-Russian science historian Alexandre Koyré, who coined the phrase "scientific revolution," and who Kuhn praised throughout *Structure*, led Kuhn down the path of historical interpretation. In Kuhn's view, the history of science had languished as a peripheral subject in both history and science departments. But Koyré's work gave it scholarly credibility.[14] Kuhn argues that Koyré paved the way for a new approach to writing history texts that can "suggest the possibility of a new image of science."[15] In other words, Kuhn believed that the findings of historical studies could revolutionize the understanding of how science works. A lively contemporary debate raged and, with the publication of *Structure*, Kuhn occupied a central position within it.

NOTES

1   Thomas S. Kuhn, "The History of Science," in *The Essential Tension: Selected Studies in Scientific Tradition and Change* (Chicago, IL: University of Chicago Press, 1977), 107

2   Peter Godfrey-Smith, *An Introduction to the Philosophy of Science: Theory and Reality* (Chicago, IL: University of Chicago Press, 2003), 5.

3   Ian Hacking, *The Social Construction of What?* (Cambridge, MA: Harvard University Press, 1999), 68.

4   Godfrey-Smith, *Theory and Reality*, 6.

5   Godfrey-Smith, *Theory and Reality*, 228.

6   Godfrey-Smith, *Theory and Reality*, 28.

7   Godfrey-Smith, *Theory and Reality*, 28.

8   Godfrey-Smith, *Theory and Reality*, 27.

9   R. N. D. Martin, *Pierre Duhem: Philosophy and History in the Work of a Believing Physicist* (La Salle, IL: Open Court, 1991), 139.

10 Thomas S. Kuhn, "Afterwords," *World Changes: Thomas Kuhn and the Nature of Science*, ed. Paul Horwich (Cambridge, MA: MIT Press, 1993).

11 Thomas S. Kuhn, *The Road Since Structure: Philosophical Essays, 1970–1993 with an Autobiographical Interview*, ed. James Conant and John Haugeland (Chicago, IL: Chicago University Press, 2000), 264.

12 Thomas S. Kuhn, *The Structure of Scientific Revolutions*, 4th ed. (Chicago, IL: University of Chicago Press, 2012), 2.

13 Kuhn, *Structure*, 3.

14 Kuhn, *Structure*, 3. In a 1971 piece he talked about Koyré as being his "maître" above all other historians; Thomas S. Kuhn, "Concepts of Cause in the Development of Physics," in *The Essential Tension*, 21 (this is the published translation of the originally French piece).

15 Kuhn, *Structure*, 3.

MODULE 4
THE AUTHOR'S CONTRIBUTION

KEY POINTS

- Thomas Kuhn argued that science followed this course: Pre-consensus science* ⊠ Normal science* ⊠ Crisis science* ⊠ Extraordinary science* ⊠ Scientific revolution.*

- *The Structure of Scientific Revolutions* overturned the dominant view of linear, cumulative progress in science by proposing this cyclical alternative.

- Although the cyclical model developed the old concept of a scientific revolution, its originality lay in the challenge it posed to objectivity (that is, the assumption that a scientist was capable of examining "reality" without his or her own world view intervening).

Author's Aims

In *The Structure of Scientific Revolutions*, Thomas Kuhn aimed to demonstrate that scientific knowledge progresses in cycles—a theory he began to develop during his doctoral studies when, as he wrote, his "exposure to out-of-date scientific theory and practice radically undermined some of my basic conceptions about the nature of science."[1]

This cyclical understanding began with an acknowledgement that historians of science had themselves framed their histories with concepts that changed over time.[2] If the analysis of history can be cyclical, then so can knowledge itself.

Kuhn demonstrated the cycles moving from "pre-consensus science"—when rival schools of thought addressed the same object from different perspectives, reaching different conclusions[3]—through stages to revolution and back again. Pre-consensus science, for Kuhn, is

> ❝ The origin of *The Structure of Scientific Revolutions* explains why the questions there raised are similar to those asked by recent converts to the history of science who have been trained as scientists and by historians strongly influenced by sociology; indeed Kuhn regards this book as a contribution to the sociology of knowledge. ❞
>
> Marie Boas Hall, review of *The Structure of Scientific Revolutions*

"something less than a science"[4] because no shared opinions exist and any idea can be tried. He cites as an example the different interpretations held by scientists in the seventeenth century, before the work of the English physicist Isaac Newton,* of how light waves behave—a domain of physics known as optics.[5]

Out of this "pre-consensus science" grows "normal science" in which one school of thought wins the allegiance of all scientists, who then work to modify agreed concepts by consensus within accepted rules of scientific practice,[6] accumulating knowledge in a linear manner.[7]

This gives way to crisis and extraordinary science and eventually revolution. A crisis in science occurs when scientists, faced with inexplicable phenomena that arise during normal science, can no longer explain the world. What Kuhn calls "science in a crisis state"[8] reconsiders the conventions and agreed concepts that direct normal science. When crises occur, several paradigms* compete for the acceptance of the scientific community.* These paradigms, in Kuhn's view, are incommensurable*—that is, they are worldviews that explain reality so differently that they cannot coexist.

Kuhn argues that it is scientists' personalities and preferences that ultimately explain the decisions scientific communities make about which paradigm will be accepted. If paradigms explain the world differently, but each is plausible according to its own argument, then choices are made for reasons that are not scientific but personal.[9]

By disrupting the linear process of normal science, these crises make scientific development uneven. They do not always end in revolution. Most often, they find a resolution. Perhaps a solution emerges from the "normal science" camp. Or perhaps the scientific community agrees to set the problem aside for future generations. But when such solutions fail, a revolution may take place. After the revolution, science reverts back to "normal science" and the whole process repeats itself.

If a scientific field reaches the revolutionary stage, the effects are dramatic. Revolutions create new paradigms, which require the complete "reconstruction" of a field of science.[10] By the end of the revolution, the profession itself will have changed its views, methods, and goals.[11]

Alluding to the psychological theory of "gestalt"*—which assumes that we build a worldview by mentally ordering our experience in such a way that some individual, new, experience has the capacity to radically alter our understanding of what is "real" altogether—Kuhn compares the change to a visual gestalt whereby an animal previously seen as a bird is now seen as an antelope.[12] The revolutionary paradigm shift* produces an equal displacement in scientists' conceptual framework.[13]

Approach

Kuhn seeks to look at science in its context, as scientists themselves have interpreted it. He says he is trying to "display the historical integrity of [a] science in its own time" by considering what is going on in the minds of a group of scientists practicing "some particular scientific specialty during some particular period."[14]

Although Kuhn attaches great importance to history as a starting point for analyzing scientific activity, this is not the end of his approach. From a historical understanding of how scientists work, he maintains that he can deduce a series of concepts explaining how and why they worked, and how they continue to work.[15]

This approach contrasts with that of logical empiricism,* according to which a scientific experiment that cannot be verified proves very little about reality. Consequently, the relationship between Kuhn's thought and that of logical empiricism, remains unclear, and Kuhn himself often avoided the comparison.[16]

Kuhn drew heavily on the work of early twentieth-century historians such as the Franco-Russian Alexandre Koyré* (coiner of the phrase "scientific revolution") and the French historian Pierre Duhem.* These scholars sought to show the true character of science by studying episodes in the history of science* in detail to see how scientists had actually worked.

Where logical empiricists explained historical science by turning first to philosophical concepts, Kuhn effectively did the reverse, putting history first to reveal philosophical concepts: "Kuhn's work seemed to show how interesting it is to connect philosophical questions about science with questions about the history of science."[17]

Contribution in Context

The originality of *The Structure of Scientific Revolutions* lies in the fact that it builds on existing frameworks for understanding the history of science—notably the idea that science occupies a special place in human intellectual enterprise—while destabilizing those same frameworks by arguing that scientific advances are cyclical and that scientists have a large say in defining "reality." When leading logical empiricists sought to assemble a definitive collection of statements about the nature, function, and purpose of science,[18] Kuhn offered to let them include *The Structure of Scientific Revolutions* in their project, the *Encyclopedia of Unified Science.*

Another highly original aspect of Kuhn's work was his subversion of existing concepts used both by logical empiricists and historians. Kuhn shocked the scientific establishment by showing that apparently settled ideas contained within them the seeds of radical reinterpretation—the polar opposite of the dream of logical empiricists to assemble a definitive collection of statements about science.

In 1985, the American philosopher Arthur Danto* said that Kuhn ensured the onset of "post-empiricism," writing that there "really was a unity of science, in the sense that all of science was brought under history rather than, as before, history having been brought under science construed on a model of physics."[19]

Kuhn's originality lay, then, in creating unity by showing the inherent disunity of science, and so moving science beyond logical empiricism.

NOTES

1   Thomas S. Kuhn, *The Structure of Scientific Revolutions*, 4th ed. (Chicago, IL: University of Chicago Press, 2012), v.

2   Kuhn, *Structure*, 2, 7; Kuhn, *The Essential Tension: Selected Studies in Scientific Tradition and Change* (Chicago, IL: University of Chicago Press, 1977), xi.

3   Kuhn, *Structure*, 4, 12–3, 47–8, 61–2, 178–9.

4   Kuhn, *Structure*, 13–8.

5   Kuhn, *Structure*, 16.

6   Kuhn, *Structure*, 17–9, 178.

7   Kuhn, *Structure*, 52–3.

8   Kuhn, *Structure*, 82–7, 101, 154.

9   Kuhn, *Structure*, 95.

10 Kuhn, *Structure,* 85.

11 Kuhn, *Structure*, 85.

12 Kuhn, *Structure*, 85.

13 Kuhn, *Structure*, 102.

14 Kuhn, *Structure*, 3.

15 Kuhn, *Structure*, 3.

16 Joseph Rouse, "Kuhn's Philosophy of Scientific Practice," in *Thomas Kuhn*, ed. Thomas Nickles (Cambridge: Cambridge University Press, 2003), 101.

17 Peter Godfrey-Smith, *An Introduction to the Philosophy of Science: Theory and Reality* (Chicago, IL: University of Chicago Press, 2003), 78.

18 Peter Novick, *The Noble Dream: The "Objectivity Question" and the American Historical Profession* (Cambridge: Cambridge University Press, 1988), 526.

19 Arthur Danto, *Narration and Knowledge* (New York: Columbia University Press, 1985), xi–ii.

SECTION 2
IDEAS

MODULE 5
MAIN IDEAS

KEY POINTS

- The main themes of T*he Structure of Scientific Revolutions* are scientific revolution,* paradigm,* and incommensurability.*

- Kuhn argues that when scientists challenge and overturn paradigms, they drive scientific progress from normal science* (that is, science practiced according to the prevailing worldview) through crisis* and revolutionary science* back to a new normal science.

- The argument first appears—as a briefer analysis—in two volumes of the *International Encyclopedia of Science.*

Key Themes

In *The Structure of Scientific Revolutions,* Thomas Kuhn constructs his original understanding of science around three key themes:

- The idea of a scientific revolution
- The concept of a paradigm
- The concept of incommensurability

As Kuhn sees it, *scientific revolution* occurs when momentous breakthroughs propel scientific progress. These breakthroughs permanently change the way scientists understand the world.

Kuhn used the word *paradigm* to refer to the core concepts scientists worked with to deepen their knowledge of the world. Kuhn's understanding of science anchors itself firmly around this core idea. He defines it as referring to any "accepted model or pattern" of scientific conduct.[1]

> ❝ Conceived as a set of instruments for solving technical puzzles in selected areas, science clearly gains in precision and scope with the passage of time. As an instrument, science undoubtedly does progress. ❞
>
> Thomas Kuhn, *The Structure of Scientific Revolutions*

The concept of *incommensurability*, closely related to paradigm, forms the last of Kuhn's core ideas. Incommensurability describes the relationship between paradigms during periods of extraordinary science,* when anomalies* (that is, observations that do not "fit" into the accepted model) cast doubt over the consensus paradigm.* In moments of crisis, when two or more paradigms compete to explain reality differently, the paradigms themselves become incommensurable—that is, scientists using different paradigms cannot communicate with one another. Even if they can, they cannot understand each others' findings because they are using the different standards of evidence or different concepts required by their preferred paradigm. This incommensurability and the chaos that results continues until a new consensus paradigm is reached.[2]

Together, these three ideas enable Kuhn to make his argument for scientific progress. He sees it as cyclical and also as determined by the community* of scientists, since scientists, by their actions, both accept and bring down paradigms.

Kuhn legitimates his ideas by basing his concepts on historical examples of scientific breakthroughs. In considering past scientific advances, he shows how his general concepts can explain and help us understand specific discoveries. He intended his work to definitively discredit the linear, cumulative understanding of science that characterizes the logical empiricist* approach to the philosophy of science.*

Exploring the Ideas

The key to Kuhn's historical reading of scientific progress lies in the notion of a scientific revolution. His argument is that "each scientific revolution alters the historical perspective of the community [of scientists] that experiences it" with the result that it "should affect the structure of post-revolutionary textbooks and research publications."[3] In other words, every time a scientific breakthrough occurs, scientists use their newfound knowledge to rewrite science. In Kuhn's view, scientific knowledge does not accumulate. Breakthroughs do not add to existing knowledge, they create a "world change" in which scientists see reality differently.[4]

In any scientific revolution, scientists must establish a suitable paradigm to explain what they study. A paradigm emerges to explain and then guide scientists' work on "a few problems that the group of practitioners has come to recognize as acute."[5] According to the German philosopher Paul Hoyningen-Huene,* Kuhn's chief interpreter and defender, paradigms gain acceptance through a two-part process. First, scientists agree that a certain situation presents a scientific problem. Then they agree on a paradigm that provides a scientifically acceptable solution.[6] Paradigms both explain scientific problems and guide scientific practice.[7] Although Kuhn describes them as relatively "rigid," being part of normal science which is itself characterized by rigidity,[8] they are not so inflexible as to cause scientists to end their "puzzle-solving" research.[9]

Scientists will continue to research and encounter new problems. Indeed, paradigms must be relatively open-ended in that they can provide the direction of future research. They help scientists determine which facts are worth gathering and analyzing.[10] Once scientists encounter a problem the paradigm cannot explain, then the concept of incommensurability (that is, the impossibility of reconciling two opposing paradigms) explains how, during a period of crisis science, and even a scientific revolution itself, potential replacement consensus paradigms are considered and discarded.

As we have seen, for Kuhn a paradigm is, fundamentally, "an accepted model or pattern."[11] Hence social acceptance in the community of scientists is essential to the establishment of a paradigm. Kuhn sees a fundamental difference between a paradigm and a rule. For him, rules in the scientific community* are secondary and reductive—and consequently not as productive as paradigms. Rules are also too rigid for scientific enterprise. In conceptualizing the idea of paradigm, Kuhn appeals to the concept of "tacit knowledge"* developed by the British Hungarian philosopher of science Michael Polanyi.* Tacit knowledge is "knowledge that is acquired through practice and ... cannot be articulated explicitly"—in other words, the unspoken guidelines scientists accept.[12]

Kuhn believes scientific paradigms have their own lifespan. They begin by solving a particularly acute problem, and end by failing to answer a subsequent anomaly of similar importance. Yet paradigms do not simply fade away; they resist change until a new paradigm takes over. The process of replacing one paradigm with another occurs in what he calls a scientific revolution—the total renewal of an entire scientific field.

This leads Kuhn to his associated thesis: that of incommensurability. Incommensurability describes the relationship between paradigms. In Kuhn's view, no more than one paradigm can ever exist in a particular field of scientific study at any given time. Paradigms hold absolute authority, dictating the entire landscape of a scientific discipline. When a paradigm takes over, "the profession will have changed its view of the field, its methods, and its goals."[13] Once scientists adopt a new paradigm, the entire "conceptual network" of the world changes in that discipline; scientists operate in a "new world."[14] Kuhn compares the competition between paradigms to the battle between revolutionary factions; the winning party essentially wins all.

To explain Kuhn's views on incommensurability, imagine that "A" represents the "world" and "B" represents the human observer.

Kuhn claims that scientists adopt paradigms before they begin the process of scientific observation. So when the observer B looks at the world A, she or he sees the shape of that world through a paradigm that she or he has already adopted. If B adopts paradigm 1, the act of observation will produce world A1. But if B adopts paradigm 2, observation will render world A2. Because the interpretation begins even before the act of observation, however, the paradigm does not determine the existence of either world. The reality of the worlds is independent of the observer.

Many readers understand incommensurability to mean a radical, complete and instantaneous "world change."[15] That understanding caused critics such as the Australian philosopher Howard Sankey* to accuse Kuhn of being suspect to "some form of idealism."*[16] Idealism holds that the human mind plays a decisive role in shaping how people see the world—people do not have direct access to reality. But this does not describe Kuhn's position: "though the world does not change with a change of paradigm," he writes, "the scientist afterward works in a different world."[17]

In statements like this, Kuhn explains that he does not mean that reality depends on the observer. He means that the sensory perception of reality depends on a previously established paradigm. In his view, science is precisely the ability to fit both theory and perception to an objective, "real" nature.[18]

Nevertheless, Kuhn appears deliberately ambiguous. He recognizes that there is a "real" world; it is simply so remote from human knowledge as to be almost inconsequential.[19] As an example, he offers the revolution in chemistry sparked by the work of the eighteenth-century French chemist Antoine Lavoisier,* the discoverer of oxygen, making the radical observation that "in the absence of some recourse to that hypothetical fixed nature that he 'saw differently,' the principle of economy will urge us to say that after discovering oxygen Lavoisier worked in a different world."[20]

For Sankey, however, these statements signify that the "real" world is "dispensable" or "irrelevant" for Kuhn, as it is essentially unattainable by scientific perception or belief.[21] Kuhn's position rests (Sankey argues) on the idea that scientists cannot access the real world and that the scientific community to which they and their paradigms belong have molded their thought.

The German philosopher Paul Hoyningen-Huene proposes a more nuanced interpretation, differentiating between the world-in-itself (the "real" world) and the phenomenal world (the world of human experience).[22] While the "real world" is independent of science, the phenomenal world, shaped by paradigms, is not—a view derived from the German philosopher Immanuel Kant,* whom Kuhn acknowledged had influenced his thought.[23]

Although Kuhn endorsed Hoyningen-Huene's Kantian interpretation, the British philosopher Alexander Bird* remained skeptical. For him, in pegging his work to Kant's, Kuhn was attempting to give "his earlier thought a (particular species of) philosophical sophistication that it did not really have."[24]

Language and Expression

Kuhn uses the words "paradigm" and "incommensurability" in different ways throughout *The Structure of Scientific Revolutions*, acknowledging that "the concept of paradigm will often substitute for a variety of familiar notions."[25]

The philosopher of science Margaret Masterman* identified 21 meanings of the term "paradigm" in *Structure of Scientific Revolutions*[26]—a linguistic fuzziness representing both a strength and a weakness. On the one hand, an idea as vague as Kuhn's paradigm is difficult for philosophers of science to accept. On the other, Kuhn's ability to condense many connected concepts into a single word would have a major impact on academia and popular culture.

Similarly, Hoyningen-Huene observes that Kuhn uses the term "incommensurability" in two different ways. Initially, it appears in Kuhn's discussion of the way problems and standards change as science goes from a pre-revolutionary to a post-revolutionary mode.[27] But when he returns to the concept later in the work, Kuhn uses the term in a much more radical way, saying: "[The] scientist's perception of his environment must be re-educated ... the world of his research will seem, here and there, incommensurable with the one he had inhabited before."[28]

Kuhn compares this phenomenon with a "gestalt switch,"* a term derived from the Gestalt school of psychology, according to which some new, individual piece of perceptual information can lead to a fundamental transformation in our understanding of what it is we are perceiving. He also cites the revolutionary way the scientific world changed after Nicolaus Copernicus* unveiled his model of the universe in the sixteenth century; "after Copernicus," he writes, "astronomers lived in a different world."[29]

NOTES

1   Thomas S. Kuhn, *The Structure of Scientific Revolutions*, 4th ed. (Chicago, IL: University of Chicago Press, 2012), 23.

2   Kuhn, *Structure*, 85.

3   Kuhn, *Structure*, VIII.

4   Kuhn, *Structure*, 19.

5   Kuhn, *Structure*, 24.

6   Paul Hoyningen-Huene, *Reconstructing Scientific Revolutions: Thomas S. Kuhn's Philosophy of Science* (Chicago, IL: University of Chicago Press, 1993), 134–5.

7   Kuhn, *Structure*, 46.

8   Kuhn, *Structure*, 19, 49, 64.

9   Kuhn, *Structure of Scientific Revolutions*, 49.

10 Kuhn, *Structure*, 25–6, 48.

11 Kuhn, *Structure*, 23.

12 Kuhn, *Structure*, 44–5 n.1.

13 Kuhn, *Structure*, 85.

14 Kuhn, *Structure*, 102.

15 Hanne Andersen, Peter Barker and Xiang Chen, *The Cognitive Structure of Scientific Revolutions* (Cambridge: Cambridge University Press, 2006), 106.

16 Howard Sankey, "Kuhn's Changing Concept of Incommensurability," *British Journal for the Philosophy of Science* 44, no. 4 (1993):

17 Kuhn, *Structure of Scientific Revolutions,* 121.

18 Kuhn, *Structure*, 134: "it is hard to make nature fit a paradigm."

19 Kuhn, *Structure*, 111.

20 Kuhn, *Structure*, 118.

21 Sankey, "Kuhn's Changing Concept of Incommensurability," 764.

22 Hoyningen-Huene, *Reconstructing Scientific Revolutions*, 239.

23 Thomas S. Kuhn, *The Road Since Structure: Philosophical Essays, 1970– 1993 with an Autobiographical Interview*, ed. James Conant and John Haugeland (Chicago, IL: Chicago University Press), 264.

24 Alexander Bird, "The Structure of Scientific Revolutions and its Significance: An Essay Review of the Fiftieth Anniversary Edition," *The British Journal for the Philosophy of Science* 63, no. 4 (2012): 869.

25 Kuhn, *Structure*, 11.

26 Margaret Masterman, "The Nature of a Paradigm," in *Criticism and the Growth of Knowledge*, ed. Imre Lakatos and A. Musgrave (Cambridge: Cambridge University Press, 1970), 59–89.

27 Kuhn, *Structure*, 103.

28 Kuhn, *Structure*, 112.

29 Kuhn, *Structure*, 117.

MODULE 6
SECONDARY IDEAS

KEY POINTS

- *The Structure of Scientific Revolutions* made valuable contributions to the sociology* of scientific communities* (that is, the study of the world of science in its social aspect), the concept of relativism* (roughly, the belief that "final" answers are impossible in science), and the plurality of natural sciences.

- These ideas derive from Kuhn's overall argument about the cyclical structure of scientific progress.

- Although it is sometimes overlooked, relativism has had the widest impact on social scientists in general. The work also changed the way historians of science think about the sociology of the scientific community and the plurality of the natural sciences.

Other Ideas

The main ideas in Thomas Kuhn's *The Structure of Scientific Revolutions* involve scientific revolution,* paradigm* and incommensurability*— compelling ideas that have produced fascinating developments of the history of science.* In addition the book also contains three important secondary ideas, each enhancing Kuhn's overriding argument about the cyclical nature of scientific advances.

First, Kuhn develops a particular idea of the relationship between the scientist and the scientific community. He looks at science as a "social enterprise," affected by the characteristics of its practitioners and "external social, economic and intellectual conditions."[1] This represents an unusual development in work on the philosophy of science.*

> ❝ Taken as a group or in groups, practitioners of the developed sciences are, I have argued, fundamentally puzzle-solvers … Like any other value, puzzle-solving ability proves equivocal in application. Two men who share it may nevertheless differ in the judgments they draw from its use. ❞
>
> Thomas Kuhn, *The Structure of Scientific Revolutions*

In Kuhn's view, science is unlike any other human activity. In this, he agrees with those who subscribe to the school of thought of logical empiricism.* But where the logical empiricists believe science to be special because it is a uniquely rational accumulation of knowledge, Kuhn believes that we arrive at knowledge in cycles, and that scientists do not merely passively process data about reality. For Kuhn, scientists have a say in what is "real" or not, according to the paradigm they actively choose.

This idea was a challenge to the logical positivism of the 1960s, notably its assumptions about rationality. But it ran the risk of being a self-contradictory argument. How could science retain the special position in human endeavor that Kuhn argued it held if it was neither objective nor a unique, linear accumulation of human knowledge? Had Kuhn tried to say that scientific activity was as subjective as any other intellectual pursuit, this contradiction would not have been an issue.

Second, Kuhn destabilizes the notion of truth in science. His argument about paradigms implies that scientists cannot reach definitive conclusions, since the paradigm is formed and accepted by a scientific community that does not have direct access to reality. This leads to him making remarks, at the end of the work, about "salvaging the notion of 'truth'."[2]

Third, Kuhn examines the pluralism of the sciences. In his view, different branches of the sciences operate with their own paradigms and have their own cyclical developments—a notion that strikes down the image of science as a unified, monolithic enterprise whose foundational principles never vary. As Kuhn sees it, each branch of scientific inquiry—from biology, chemistry, and physics to more specialized sub-disciplines—has its own communities with their own paradigms; scientists and science vary by field and object of research.

Exploring the Ideas

Kuhn sees the scientific community as a closed unit, separate from society, pursuing its own agenda. Once scientists debate and adopt a paradigm they begin to use an "esoteric* language"—an exotic vocabulary unintelligible to the general public.[3]

Scientists could choose to pursue noble goals that would benefit the "welfare of mankind."[4] Instead, Kuhn sees them looking inward, intent only on improving and cultivating their reputations. Kuhn explains that "unlike the engineer, and many doctors, and most theologians, the scientist need not choose problems because they urgently need solution;"[5] instead, "many of the greatest scientific minds have devoted all of their professional attention to demanding puzzles of this sort. On most occasions any field of specialization offers nothing else to do, a fact that makes it no less fascinating to the proper sort of addict."[6]

In this way, Kuhn blew apart the old understanding of scientists as a venerable community serving mankind. It opened the scientific sphere to the attention of sociologists of science. By arguing that scientists and non-scientists were the same, he implied that their social interactions demanded the same scrutiny.[7] In making this argument, he insisted nevertheless that science itself differed from other human endeavors.

The absence of consensual agreement—the paradigm—voids science: "Once a first paradigm through which to view nature has been found, there is no such thing as research in the absence of any paradigm. To reject one paradigm without simultaneously substituting another is to reject science itself."[8] Although social scientists later deployed this notion in other fields, this was not Kuhn's purpose. For him, the paradigm was a definitive attribute of science.

Kuhn's destabilization of notions of truth also related to the paradigm concept. In his view, no paradigm can ever explain reality as it truly exists. Eventually every paradigms falls, making way for a new one, leaving nothing of any permanence in scientific conclusions but creating continual progress.[9]

This concept gave rise to the idea of relativism, which holds that scientific knowledge has no universal validity. Instead, scientific knowledge relates to the state of scientific development at any given time. As Kuhn wrote, "to be admirably successful is never, for a scientific theory, to be completely successful."[10] In Kuhn's paradoxical narrative, the more precise the paradigm is, the more likely it is to fail. Anomalies* become much more evident against a background of increased precision. Such "technical breakdown" induces crises in normal science.*[11] We have, therefore, to "relinquish the notion, explicit or implicit, that changes of paradigm carry scientists and those who learn from them closer and closer to the truth."[12]

During periods of normal science, fundamental progress occurs as research makes numerous discoveries using the consensus paradigm.* Kuhn believes that this is a natural consequence of the entire scientific community being in consensus. Thus, "the reception of a common paradigm [frees] the scientific community from the need constantly to re-examine its first principles." Its members can therefore focus their attention "upon the subtlest and most esoteric of the phenomena that concerns it."[13] In this respect, progress can be defined as an increase in precision that improves on the original paradigm.

Yet, surprisingly, there is a sense in which progress across paradigms is possible. As Kuhn sees it, a paradigm never completely erases the previous paradigm's findings. On the contrary, new paradigms "usually preserve a great deal of the most concrete parts of past achievement and they always permit additional concrete problem-solutions besides."[14] Implicitly, a sense of progress arises as new developments incorporate older ones. As Kuhn puts it, scientific development is an enterprise characterized "by an increasingly detailed and refined understanding of nature."[15]

To clarify his point, Kuhn uses the analogy of Darwinian* selection. He describes the English naturalist Charles Darwin's* biological work in the nineteenth century as fundamentally a movement away from teleology* (the idea that development occurs towards a pre-decided goal) to an understanding of the natural world as the result of unplanned progress that can be measured only against its earlier incarnations. The result is increased "articulation and specialization" but no clear goal.[16] Remarkably, Kuhn never set aside this analogy with Darwinian evolution, even in his late works.

Kuhn's relativism also links to the process by which scientists choose paradigms. Once science is in crisis and competing theories emerge, the success of a paradigm "can never be unequivocally settled by logic and experiment alone."[17] Instead, it relies on such factors as persuasion, power struggles amongst junior and senior scientists, individual scientists' support from university administration, and the availability of funding and financial support for research. Kuhn makes it clear in *The Structure of Scientific Revolutions* that paradigms do not succeed because they are *true* but ultimately because the dominant factions within the scientific community choose one paradigm over another.

Alluding to the novel *1984*, the English writer George Orwell's* vision of a future in which individuality has been erased, Kuhn writes that a newcomer to a scientific community is "like the typical character of ... *1984*, the victim of a history rewritten by the powers that be."[18] He or she is not trained to question the paradigm, but to accept it; in this sense, in scientific communities education basically acts as an "initiation."[19]

Nevertheless, Kuhn builds his argument for the plurality of science on the temporary nature of paradigms, and the fact that different branches of science use different paradigms. Kuhn wants to arrive at foundational concepts underpinning the history of all science. But he maintains that scientists have the power to choose which paradigms they use and when.[20] In this sense, the success of a paradigm "can never be unequivocally settled by logic and experiment alone." This confirms that scientists' views and preferences play their part in the course of science.[21] Kuhn implicitly rejects grand concepts of unified science and theories of everything, wondering "whether truth in the sciences can ever be one."[22] Scientific revolutions occur within specialized traditions and do not need to apply to others.[23]

In the seventeenth century, scientists made many of the discoveries about gravity and the laws of motion we now take for granted. That was undoubtedly a grand scientific revolution. But Kuhn believes that scientific revolutions do not need to be so sweeping. For him, they come in different shapes and sizes, including both well-known "revolutions" such as that of the French chemist Antoine Lavoisier,* who discovered the existence of oxygen, or the less well-known discovery of the X-ray.[24]

All of these revolutions have one thing in common in Kuhn's view: they all break down and replace an existing paradigm.[25]

Overlooked

Scholars have often overlooked the psychological and cognitive points Kuhn makes in *Structure*.[26]

His social analyses of community affairs overshadow his discussion of the "changes in perception" in Gestalt* psychology. The British historian of science Alexander Bird* notes that Kuhn knew more about psychology than sociology:[27] "[The] time has come to reappraise those naturalistic elements of Kuhn's thought that he himself abandoned such as the psychological nature of a scientific revolution and a psychological rather than linguistic notion of incommensurability."[28] Bird specifically referred to cognitive science* as providing tools for such analyses. But he did not elaborate on this idea.

Scholars working on the (overlooked) concepts of cognitive science in Kuhn's work include the philosophers of science Hanne Andersen,* Peter Barker,* and Xiang Chen*[29]; all have focused on Kuhn's less-discussed endorsement of the philosopher Ludwig Wittgenstein's* theory of "family resemblance." Wittgenstein argued that objects seemingly connected by one common feature may actually have a series of overlapping features tying them together[30]—that idea lay behind Kuhn's notion of a paradigm. According to Andersen, Barker and Chen, Kuhn was the only philosopher of science in the English-speaking world to adopt and interact with this idea before the mid-1970s.[31]

NOTES

1 Thomas S. Kuhn, *The Structure of Scientific Revolutions*, 4th ed. (Chicago, IL: University of Chicago Press, 2012), x.

2 Kuhn, *Structure*, 206.

3 Kuhn, *Structure*, 20–1.

4 Kuhn, *Structure*, 37.

5 Kuhn, *Structure*, 163.

6 Kuhn, *Structure*, 38.

7 Kuhn, *Structure*, 40.

8 Kuhn, *Structure*, 79.

9 Alexander Bird, *Thomas Kuhn* (Chesham: Acumen, 2000), 3–9.

10 Kuhn, *Structure*, 68.

11 Kuhn, *Structure*, 69.

12 Kuhn, *Structure*, 160.

13 Kuhn, *Structure*, 163.

14 Kuhn, *Structure*, 168.

15 Kuhn, *Structure*, 169.

16 Kuhn, *Structure*, 171.

17 Kuhn, *Structure*, 95.

18 Kuhn, *Structure*, 166.

19 Kuhn, *Structure*, 164.

20 Kuhn, *Structure*, 50.

21 Kuhn, *Structure*, 95.

22 Kuhn, *Structure*, 167.

23 Kuhn, *Structure*, 50–1.

24 Kuhn, *Structure*, 93.

25 Kuhn, *Structure*, 92.

26 Alexander Bird, "*The Structure of Scientific Revolutions*: An Essay Review of the Fiftieth Anniversary Edition," *British Journal for the Philosophy of Science* 63, no. 4 (2012): 865.

27 Bird, "*The Structure of Scientific Revolutions*," 7–8.

28 Bird, *Thomas Kuhn*, 14.

29 Hanne Andersen, Peter Barker and Xiang Chen, *The Cognitive Structure of Scientific Revolutions* (Cambridge: Cambridge University Press, 2006), 12–8.

30 Nancy Nersessian, "Kuhn, Conceptual Change and Cognitive Science," in *Thomas Kuhn*, ed. Thomas Nickles (Cambridge: Cambridge University Press, 2003), 180.

31 Andersen, Barker and Chen, *The Cognitive Structure*, 8; Nersessian, "Kuhn and Cognitive Science," 1.

MODULE 7
ACHIEVEMENT

KEY POINTS

- *The Structure of Scientific Revolutions* achieved Thomas Kuhn's aim of historically re-examining the natural sciences.

- The rise in externalist* readings of science and of sociology* (according to which politics, economics and culture play a significant role in scientific advancement) did most to assist Kuhn's widespread success.

- Scholarly misunderstandings of Kuhn's work hampered his ability to convey his argument to a wide audience.

Assessing the Argument

Thomas Kuhn's *The Structure of Scientific Revolutions* chiefly aimed to challenge the view of science as a rational* exercise that continuously increases the quantity of human knowledge.[1]

Although it has been argued that Kuhn also wanted to bring about the demise of the philosophy of logical empiricism,* the science historians Michael Friedman* and George A. Reisch* have shown that he had strong ties with the empiricists.[2] Indeed, Kuhn's work shows astonishing similarities with that of the German logical-empiricist Rudolf Carnap.*[3] So it is accurate to say that while Kuhn's essentially historical view challenged the logical-empiricist mainstream of scholarship on the history and philosophy of science,* he accepted some of the central theoretical features of this "textbook tradition."

Seeing himself as the voice of the latest winning scientific faction,[4] Kuhn hoped his alternative point-of-view would free the history of science* from the assumption that its only role was to reflect philosophy.

> 66 Kuhn's book was clearly and powerfully written, filled with persuasive examples, devoid of arcane vocabulary and symbols which had made philosophy of science a closed book to most laymen. Kuhn's ideas were quickly taken up by scholars in fields far removed from the natural sciences. 99
>
> Peter Novick, *That Noble Dream*

Uncovering Kuhn's true aims in his book is a much more difficult task than it appears at first glance; although he clearly states that he wants to attack the "textbook tradition" his intentions beyond that are not always apparent. This ambiguity has led critics to various interpretations. In the revolutionary era of the 1960s, many were willing to understand Kuhn as a radical and subversive thinker. Although he disavowed such portrayals, many passages appear to encourage such a reading. When the book was first published it made a revolutionary contrast to the dogmatic rigidity of mainstream scientific textbooks.[5]

We can see today that Kuhn's work produced profound changes in our understanding of science. But it is difficult to disentangle our knowledge of those changes from what Kuhn intended when he was writing the book. Although Kuhn challenged the common assumptions regarding science in his period, he may not have intended to challenge science itself—which is what eventually happened.[6]

In challenging the older, cumulative understanding of science, Kuhn certainly demonstrated that science is cyclical. But it remains difficult to claim that he accomplished anything more. Part of this difficulty stems from the vagueness of some of Kuhn's key concepts ("paradigm,"* for example). In addition, his work became so quickly and thoroughly adopted by social scientists and historians of science that it makes it difficult to imagine any pre-Kuhnian model for understanding the history and development of science.

Achievement in Context

In the mid-twentieth century, universities increased their exploration of "externalist" readings of science and its place in society by paying attention to the greater social context in which scientific research occurs. The historian Richard Hofstadter's* work *Social Darwinism in American Thought 1860–1915* (1944) is a classic externalist examination. Hofstadter explored how the phrases "survival of the fittest" and "the struggle for existence" had emerged from the evolutionary biology of Charles Darwin,* entered into social commentary, and fed back into scientific practice in unexpected ways.[7] This trend certainly contributed to the success of *The Structure of Scientific Revolutions*, feeding the widespread interest that greeted the book when it was published.

In this regard, mention must be made of sociology—a field particularly concerned with the ways in which science and ideas have been historically shaped by social conditions. The historian of science James Marcum,* for example, believes that no discipline did more than sociology to support Kuhn's work, not least because of the way Kuhn examined the scientific community* as a social group,[8] looking within that community for the causes and characteristics of science.

In addition, *The Structure of Scientific Revolutions* appeared just as public debate about the use of atomic bombs in World War II* became more widespread. Kuhn, who had been affected by this issue during his youth, wrote *Structure* during the height of the Cold War* at a time when anyone who critiqued science from a social or externalist viewpoint risked arousing suspicions of communist* tendencies; many professors holding (or suspected of holding) such views lost their jobs.[9]

Kuhn represented a generation of new academics willing to shake up the scientific status quo and question the mainstream view of science as objective and certain. The time was ripe for this debate. As the British science interpreter Ziauddin Sardar* and the Canadian philosopher of science Ian Hacking* have pointed out, during the 1960s the public and the intellectual community began to question the role scientists, such as Kuhn's early mentor James Bryant Conant,* had played in creating atomic weapons.[10] In this sense, Kuhn's work marked a profound shift in the way we view science in society.

Structure has served as a springboard for new ideas about science. It marks an important milestone in the development of new scholarly and intellectual movements that have made science a function of scientists' social and intellectual backgrounds.[11] These thinkers questioned modern science in entirely new ways, emphasizing it as a product of a specific geographical area (Western Europe), a specific civilization (Judeo-Christian), and a specific gender (male). Some even questioned science's claim to truth and knowledge.

Many of these ideas surprised Kuhn and some caused him concern. He had never imagined that his work had the potential to spark a wide-ranging re-evaluation of science and non-science subjects, such as the sociology of knowledge. The set of analytical tools his work provided found far wider applications than he could have anticipated.

As Sardar points out, *Structure* was primarily interested in the internal reform of science. Kuhn upheld science's autonomy from society. In his subsequent interventions to "correct" the misconceptions generated by his book, Kuhn aimed to insulate science from public scrutiny.[12] In fact, the American philosopher Steve Fuller* accused *Structure* of promoting conservative forms of scholarship and perpetuating preconceptions of the special nature of science. Fuller argued that some have used the text to marginalize radical philosophies of science. Two examples of this are the philosophies promoted by the scholars Jerry Ravetz* and Paul Feyerabend,* both of whom argued that science results entirely from the predilections and preferences of individual scientists acting without reference to or desire to form part of a community.*[13]

Limitations

Despite *Structure*'s continued and extraordinary popularity, it is worthwhile considering its limitations. Foremost among these is the work's defense of the special status bestowed on science by successive governments and societies in the twentieth century—a defense based on assumptions Kuhn inherited from the school in the philosophy of science known as logical empiricism.*

If Kuhn is right, however, and scientific knowledge is not wholly objective, being a product of the community that produced it, how then can it deserve or retain that special status? Stripped of it, science would be subject to the financial pressures of restricted university funding and the lure of financial rewards. How then will scientific research maintain its rigor? Pharmaceutical corporations offer high rewards for scientists who can come up with new drug compounds. Does this skew the research agenda in the scientific community? Kuhn did not consider these implications.

In addition, Kuhn offers only a preliminary exploration of the ways in which the scientific community shapes scientific practice. There is no discussion of the possible fragility of the social structures inside the scientific community in the face of a turbulent modern economy—as was exposed in the oil crisis of 1973,* when mounting oil prices brought economic instability. For example, universities faced tough choices over increasingly scarce resources, which affected the social aspects of the academic environment. But although the internal culture of the scientific community is not as stable as Kuhn seems to assume, differing over time and across territory,[14] readers will not find this factored into Kuhn's account. As a result, the historical analysis on which rest his concepts of paradigm and incommensurability* remains incomplete, as the special status science once enjoyed recedes.[15]

NOTES

1   Thomas S. Kuhn, *The Structure of Scientific Revolutions*, 4th ed. (Chicago, IL: University of Chicago Press, 2012), x.

2   Michael Friedman, "Kuhn and Logical Empiricism," in *Thomas Kuhn*, ed. Thomas Nickles (Cambridge: Cambridge University Press, 2003), 19–21; George A. Reisch, "Did Kuhn Kill Logical Empiricism?," *Philosophy of Science* 58 (1991): 266–7.

3   Gurol Irzik and Teo Grunberg, "Carnap and Kuhn: Arch Enemies or Close Allies?," *British Journal for the Philosophy of Science* 46, no. 3 (1995): 305.

4   Kuhn, *Structure*, 135–8.

5   Kuhn, *Structure*, 166.

6   Peter Godfrey-Smith, *An Introduction to the Philosophy of Science: Theory and Reality* (Chicago, IL: University of Chicago Press, 2003), 99.

7   Richard Hoftstadter, *Social Darwinism in American Thought, 1860–1915* (Boston, MA: Beacon, 1944), 6.

8   James A. Marcum, *Thomas Kuhn's Revolution: An Historical Philosophy of Science* (London: Continuum, 2005), 142.

9   Ziauddin Sardar, "Thomas Kuhn and the Science Wars," in *Postmodernism and Big Science*, ed. Richard Appignanesi (Cambridge: Icon Books, 2002), 197.

10 Sardar, "Thomas Kuhn and the Science Wars," 195; Hacking, "Introductory Essay," in Kuhn, *Structure*, ix.

11 Sardar, "Thomas Kuhn and the Science Wars," in *Postmodernism and Big Science*, 211–21.

12 Sardar, "Thomas Kuhn and the Science Wars," 221–4.

13 Steve Fuller, *Thomas Kuhn: A Philosophical History for Our Times* (Chicago, IL: University of Chicago Press, 2000), 212.

14 John M. Ziman, *Real Science: What It Is and What it Means* (Cambridge: Cambridge University Press, 2000), 4–5.

15 Ziman, *Real Science*, 1.

MODULE 8
PLACE IN THE AUTHOR'S WORK

KEY POINTS

- Thomas Kuhn's work focused on the historical interpretation of scientific practice, with significant sociological* and philosophical speculation about underlying principles of scientific practice.

- *The Structure of Scientific Revolutions*, Kuhn's second book, set the trajectory for his later research.

- Kuhn's best-known, most widely debated and most-criticized work remains *The Structure of Scientific Revolutions*.

Positioning

It took Thomas Kuhn 15 years to write *The Structure of Scientific Revolutions*,[1] his second book. His first, *The Copernican Revolution* (1957), stemmed from his research into classical mechanics* (the physical laws concerning motion and forces as they were laid out before the twentieth century) and lacked the originality displayed in *Structure*.

In 1956, reviewing Kuhn's description of the yet-unpublished *The Copernican Revolution* on his fellowship application form, Harvard University's Tenure Committee deemed the work less a contribution to scientific knowledge than an attempt to popularize science.[2] He did not win tenure (the security of a permanent academic position). Containing early versions of ideas that would become central to *The Structure of Scientific Revolutions* and Kuhn's later work, the book nevertheless interests Kuhn scholars.

In the sixteenth century the Polish astronomer Nicolaus Copernicus* formulated the theory that the sun, rather than the earth,

> 66 One of the primary forms of what is sometimes referred to as 'historicism,' sometimes as 'relativism,' is Thomas S. Kuhn's *The Structure of Scientific Revolutions.* Although Professor Kuhn has frequently insisted that most such interpretations of his views have distorted his meaning, it is not entirely clear that he has successfully answered those of his critics who have thus interpreted his work, nor has he clarified his position so that the matter is no longer open to debate. 99
>
> Maurice Mandelbaum, "A Note on Thomas S. Kuhn's *The Structure of Scientific Revolutions*"

sat at the center of the universe. For centuries, people had assumed that the success of this worldview depended on Copernicus's unique insights in the field of astronomy. Kuhn argued, however, that the social and intellectual climate in which Copernicus wrote also played a central role.[3] In researching his book, Kuhn was able to make a case study of revolutionary thought—a mindset that would become central to the idea of "extraordinary science"* in *The Structure of Scientific Revolutions.*

A second major component of Kuhn's scheme of scientific development in *The Structure of Scientific Revolutions* concerns the idea of normal science.* Kuhn first expressed this idea in the article "The Function of Measurement in Modern Physical Science" (1961). Here he presented normal science as a process of applying the gains made in scientific revolutions* to the practice of everyday science, arguing that "the function of measurement and the source of its special appeal are derived largely from myth."[4]

Kuhn had also already introduced the notion of the paradigm* in "The Essential Tension," a paper presented in 1959 at the University of Utah Research Conference.[5]

Integration

Despite his extensive body of subsequent work, *The Structure of Scientific Revolutions*, particularly its first edition of 1962, defines Kuhn today, creating an enduring vision of its author as a radical. Intellectual and popular circles have continued to feed this myth. But although the imagery and rhetoric in the first edition of *Structure* do seem radical, recent scholarship has shown that Kuhn later modified, dismantled, and underplayed many claims and implications in the work.

Overall, and throughout his published works, Kuhn maintains the same intention: to re-assess in historical perspective and with reference to the scientific community* how science has changed and developed. His emphasis on the non-scientific aspects of science and on the historical dynamics of scientific development never changed. Nor did his commitment to the idea of paradigm and the thesis of incommensurability,* despite heavy and sustained criticism. But the seemingly radical language in the first edition of *The Structure of Scientific Revolutions* contrasts with Kuhn's later writings.[6]

Scholars still debate this point: did Kuhn retreat from a radical position after his clashes with philosophers of science? Or did the revolutionary tone of his rhetoric overstate his intentions?

Significance

The Structure of Scientific Revolutions made Kuhn famous. It quickly became an influential text not only for the history and philosophy of science* but for other disciplines as well. And although Kuhn spent much of his career after 1970 clarifying aspects that he felt critics had misunderstood,[7] he continued to believe that *The Structure of Scientific Revolutions* remained his best work.[8]

After *Structure*, Kuhn turned to research in pure history of science,* which he pursued into the late 1970s. *Black-Body Theory and the Quantum Discontinuity, 1894–1912* (1978) was a straightforward historical analysis and made no mention of the ideas of *Structure*.[9] He discussed some of the work of the early twentieth–century German theoretical physicist* Max Planck.* Critics had long viewed Planck's 1900 and 1901 papers on quantum physics* as having catalyzed the transition from classical to quantum mechanics.* Kuhn took the opposite view,[10] however, arguing that Planck had in fact never shed his classical mechanics* worldview.

In hindsight, Kuhn believed *Black-Body Theory* to have been his best work on a specifically historical subject. Historians, philosophers, and physicists, however, did not agree, some bemoaning the fact that Kuhn did not use the framework he laid out in *The Structure of Scientific Revolutions*.[11] In response to the criticism, Kuhn added an afterword in a revised edition that sought to clarify the relationship of this work to the ideas in *Structure*.[12]

After 1978, Kuhn returned once more to the concept of incommensurability, this time looking at it through the framework of linguistics. In doing so, he sought to distance himself from Gestalt psychology* and its theories of perception. According to Gestalt psychology, individuals construct their perceptions—how they see, respond to, and interact with the world—around a theoretical framework based on their beliefs. Kuhn thought the connection people had made between his theories and Gestalt had led people to misunderstand his views of incommensurability. Too many scholars saw him as arguing that scientists simply construct competing paradigms without reference to reality. In this scenario, the incommensurability of paradigms could appear to derive solely from people's arguments.

Kuhn wanted to reverse scholars' misinterpretation of his work, so he set about lecturing on areas of *Structure* that had caused confusion. For example, although he never published a book on the topic, he lectured on the idea that links exist between scientific knowledge of reality and the structure of language.[13] His theory was that a scientific paradigm is linked to a vocabulary of concepts and terms specific to that paradigm. But this vocabulary is also specific to the field of science and the scientific community in which it operates. So scientists working in different fields, and using separate paradigms, cannot borrow from other paradigms to assist each other in their research or to collaborate because the scientific vocabulary and conceptual framework of all paradigms is unique. This is why there is so much plurality within "science"—in reality, singular science is a collection of sub-disciplines and communities of scientists each with their own paradigms.[14]

In 1977 Kuhn further expanded his ideas on the incommensurability thesis by discussing in detail the way scientists choose which paradigm to adopt as the consensus—a process he labeled "theory choice." He thought the concept was ripe for further explanation after becoming aware of *Structure*'s shortcomings. In particular, he had not addressed this question: "If scientists ultimately chose a consensus paradigm* for reasons other than purely scientific considerations, could their choice be irrational?"

Wanting to avoid the implication of irrationality,* because it clashed with his intention to preserve science as an autonomous, special activity,[15] Kuhn re-asserted and elaborated on five scientific considerations that guide those in the scientific community with the power and authority to decide on a consensus paradigm:

- Accuracy
- Consistency
- Breadth of scope
- Simplicity
- Fruitfulness[16]

So although sociological features of the scientific community decided which scientists had the power to choose the consensus paradigm, scientific considerations molded their final choice.

NOTES

1   Thomas S. Kuhn, *The Structure of Scientific Revolutions*, 4th ed. (Chicago, IL: University of Chicago Press, 2012), xxxix.

2   James A. Marcum, *Thomas Kuhn's Revolution: An Historical Philosophy of Science* (London: Continuum, 2005), 13–4.

3   Thomas S. Kuhn, *The Copernican Revolution: Planetary Astronomy in the Development of Western Thought* (Cambridge, MA: Harvard University Press, 1957), VIII.

4   Thomas S. Kuhn, "The Function of Measurement in Modern Physical Science," in *The Essential Tension: Selected Studies in Scientific Tradition and Change* (Chicago, IL: Chicago UP, 1979), 161.

5   Thomas S. Kuhn, "The Essential Tension" in *The Essential Tension,* 18–26.

6   Peter Novick, *The Noble Dream: The "Objectivity Question" and the American Historical Profession* (Cambridge: Cambridge University Press, 1988), 526–8.

7   Thomas S. Kuhn, *The Road Since Structure: Philosophical Essays, 1970–1993 with an Autobiographical Interview*, ed. James Conant and John Haugeland (Chicago, IL: Chicago University Press, 2000), 7.

8   Marcum, *Thomas Kuhn's Revolution*, 109.

9   Thomas S. Kuhn, *Black Body Theory and Quantum Discontinuity, 1894–1912* (Chicago, IL: Chicago UP, 1978).

10   See Marcum's short and useful summary of this work in *Thomas Kuhn's Revolution*, 108–12.

11   Marcum, *Thomas Kuhn's Revolution*, 109.

12   See Kuhn, *Black Body Theory* 2nd ed. (1987), 349–79.

13   Marcum, *Thomas Kuhn's Revolution*, 24.

14   Howard Sankey, "Kuhn's Changing Concept of Incommensurability," *British Journal for the Philosophy of Science* 44, no. 4 (1993): 770–2 describes the changes in Kuhn's theory of incommensurability.

15   Kuhn, "Objectivity, Value Judgement and Theory Choice," in *The Essential Tension*: 321–2.

16   Kuhn, "Objectivity, Value Judgement and Theory Choice," 330–9.

SECTION 3
IMPACT

THE FIRST RESPONSES

KEY POINTS

- Critics initially focused on Kuhn's concepts of paradigm*
  and incommensurability,* the relativism* they perceived
  in his work (that is, roughly, the notion that "perfect"
  knowledge is impossible to achieve), and the image of the
  scientific community* he presented.

- The most influential criticism came from the philosophers
  Dudley Shapere* and Karl Popper,* who seized on the
  lack of precision in Kuhn's concept of paradigm. Popper
  in particular attacked Kuhn's understanding of scientific
  progress as cyclical.

- Many of the earliest responses were shaped by the cultural
  and political status of science as part of a free society in
  the Cold War.*

Criticism

In the first two years after its appearance, Thomas Kuhn's *The Structure of Scientific Revolutions* received positive reviews. After 1964, critical voices began to appear, chiefly from philosophers of science. Critics concentrated on three aspects, focusing on the term "paradigm" (and, by association, the way *Structure* portrayed science and the scientific community), what they perceived as the text's relativism, and idealism.*

In 1964, the philosopher of science Dudley Shapere criticized Kuhn for his definition of paradigm, deeming the notion too imprecise.[1] He also had trouble with Kuhn's suggestion that a paradigm shift* could alter the actual meaning of a scientific concept such as "mass." He thought instead it might alter how that notion would be

❞ 'Look,' Thomas Kuhn said. The word was weighted with weariness, as if Kuhn was resigned to the fact that I would misinterpret him, but he was still going to try—no doubt in vain—to make his point. 'Look,' he said again. He leaned his gangly frame and long face forward, and his big lower lip, which ordinarily curled up amiably at the corners, sagged. 'For Christ's sake, if I had my choice of having written the book or not having written it, I would choose to have written it. But there have certainly been aspects involving considerable upset about the response to it.' ❟

John Horgan, *The End of Science*

applied.[2] Finally, Shapere found the ideas of incommensurability and paradigm impossible to square. Understanding incommensurability to mean complete "world change," Shapere noted that paradigms could not really disagree among themselves.[3]

The influential Austrian British philosopher Karl Popper also criticized Kuhn for the lack of precision in his term "paradigm." At a 1965 seminar at the London School of Economics, Popper and his followers clashed with Kuhn.[4] The pro-Popper philosophers of science, who included Kuhn's Berkeley colleague Paul Feyerabend,* pilloried Kuhn. But it is difficult to know how much this argument impacted on Kuhn's reputation at large. Since, as one commentator observed, in 1965 "both Kuhn's and Popper's views on *science* were probably known more by reputation than readership,"[5] the discussion likely never included more than a small group of scholars. In Popper's view, science by its nature had revolutionary qualities. Its fundamental characteristics included "bold conjectures" and constant retesting and refutations of its theories.[6] Popper and others at the conference disagreed profoundly with Kuhn's division of science into "normal" and "extraordinary." For them, as Kuhn's interpreter and defender Paul Hoyningen-Huene* points out, science is an enterprise "molded by the persistent awareness of the fallibility of human epistemic claims."[7]

Popper went on to decry Kuhn's idea of normal science* as a "danger to science and indeed to our civilization."[8] In Popper's view, the dogmatic character of Kuhn's ideas was profoundly unscientific.[9] Although Popper acknowledged that dogmatic enterprise existed, he saw "normal science" as a contradiction in terms.[10] Followers of Popper also remained dissatisfied with Kuhn's depiction of the scientific community. Believing science to be fundamentally open, they harshly criticized Kuhn for describing it as "a closed society whose chief characteristic is 'the abandonment of critical discourse.'"[11]

The strongest criticism raised by philosophers of science was that Kuhn supported irrationality* and relativism. As the scholars Vasso Kindi* and Theodore Arabatzis,* interpreters and editors of Kuhn's work, have recently pointed out, these philosophers feared that Kuhn's argument was overly broad. Kuhn had said that considerations outside the scope of scientific knowledge (the professional rivalries and power struggles of the scientific community and the personal views of scientists, for example) determined the methods and conclusions of scientific knowledge. Many philosophers feared this went too far.[12] They disliked Kuhn's argument in principle because it compromised the claims of science to stand above scholarly disputes in a realm of unquestionable objectivity.

As Popper saw it, Kuhn was arguing that scientists could not rationally decide which framework to follow.[13] The Hungarian philosopher of science Imre Lakatos* accused Kuhn of proposing a view of scientific change characterized by the views of "mob psychology." He also decried Kuhn's view of paradigm change as a "mystical conversion, which is not and cannot be governed by rules of reason."[14]

Responses

Very sensitive to the criticism of his peers, Kuhn responded by delivering papers at academic conferences in London (1965), his Swarthmore Lecture (also in London, 1967) and at the Urbana conference in 1969.[15] He maintained that he had not intended to uphold relativism and irrationality. In a long response, he affirmed that science "is our surest example of sound knowledge." He also expressed his belief in the progress of science, albeit not according to the traditional perspective.[16]

As in *The Structure of Scientific Revolutions*, he sought to clarify this idea by making analogies with evolution. Charles Darwin* theorized that the fitness of a species determines its continued survival. Just as in Darwin's evolution, scientific evolution moves with no clear goal, irreversibly, in only one direction. Kuhn particularly rejected the idea that scientific development brings knowledge closer to the truth.[17]

Additionally, Kuhn strongly defended the concept of normal science in both a descriptive and normative* sense (that is, telling the reader how science ought to be rather than how it actually was). He claimed that we can detect revolutionary science* only against the background of normal science. He also maintained that the static state of normal science served to deepen scientific research and progress. In a provocative essay published in 1963, before his 1965 confrontation with Karl Popper and his supporters, Kuhn had defended the function and importance of "dogma" for scientific research. He later abandoned the use of this word due to its negative connotations.[18]

Kuhn also made great efforts to clarify the notion of the paradigm—a concept that critics had viewed as everything from unclear to downright incoherent. He admitted that his initial use of the term had been too vague, and that the "excessive plasticity" of the term "paradigm" in *The Structure of Scientific Revolutions* had led to inappropriate applications of the notion to other disciplines, particularly sociology.[19] He sought to clarify the term by dividing it into a "broad" and a "narrow" sense, likening the broad sense to a disciplinary matrix* (the symbolic generalizations, models, values, and problem solutions employed by a scientific community[20]) and the narrow sense to the solutions to concrete problems.

The German philosopher of science Paul Hoyningen-Huene observed that Kuhn stopped using the term disciplinary matrix in his later work, as he focused on the notion of the exemplar*—the idea that during periods of normal science, scientists' solutions to particular problems become well-known as models ("exemplars") of conduct under the consensus paradigm.*[21] Another change involved Kuhn's realization that "paradigm" could refer both to universal consensus and the internal consensus of certain schools of thought.

Kuhn also tried to clarify the concept of incommensurability, wanting to discourage radical understandings of the notion. In the initial edition of *Structure*, Kuhn offered a somewhat ambiguous explanation of incommensurability as "world changes." This caused readers to assume that Kuhn intended a paradigm shift to imply the complete displacement of a conceptual framework.[22] In fact, Kuhn later claimed that he never meant an entire conceptual framework change—only some theories, terms, vocabularies, or languages.[23] Communication remains possible, then, but it is only partial.

This approach led Kuhn to further emphasize language and translation problems.[24] At this point he referred to the work of the philosopher of science V. O. Quine,* whose theory of indeterminacy asserted that translations could never be perfect.[25] Kuhn used Quine's argument to show that translation of all terms across paradigms is incomplete. At the same time, some terms remained the same, and this was where communication could continue.

Kuhn intended these modifications to clarify that the choice of a new theory is not fundamentally irrational; some aspects, he proposed, remained apt for comparison. Among these were empirical* predictions and assertions about specific situations (that is, predictions and assertions based on observable evidence and rational deductions), and the comparison of two competing theories.[26] He strongly denied that incommensurability and incomparability were the same thing.[27]

Conflict and Consensus

Although the modifications Kuhn made to *The Structure of Scientific Revolutions* dramatically transformed his work, they did not appease all of his critics, many of whom saw Kuhn's clarifications as a new and less radical theory.[28]

The philosopher of science John Worrall,* who had studied under Imre Lakatos, criticized Kuhn's concession on the subject of progress. Worrall argued that watering down the concept of incommensurability detracted from his overall argument.[29] Kuhn remained adamant, however, that he intended his explanations to clarify—not modify—his ideas.

Some critics were not completely appeased by the revised edition of *Structure* that Kuhn published in 1970. The philosophers of science Alan Musgrave* and Dudley Shapere, for example, remained unconvinced by Kuhn's use of a disciplinary matrix and exemplar to explain paradigms.[30] Shapere, arguably Kuhn's strongest critic, felt that Kuhn had not successfully defended himself against the charge of relativism.[31] The underlying problem derived from the first edition of *Structure*, in which Kuhn's key concepts such as paradigm, so Shapere believed, remained obscure. And one cannot produce an intelligible concept by further explaining the nonsensical.[32]

The controversy surrounding *The Structure of Scientific Revolutions* did not die down quickly. Although it became less heated in the following years, Kuhn continued to be the subject of criticism, especially from philosophers of science. Kuhn even angered his own supporters, particularly radical scholars and thinkers, displeased by his later retractions.

Nevertheless, he remained adamant that writing *Structure* proved a timely contribution to the history and philosophy of science,* commenting when interviewed that "if I had my choice of having written the book or not having written it, I would choose to have written it. But there have certainly been aspects involving considerable upset about the response to it."[33]

NOTES

1   Dudley Shapere, "The Structure of Scientific Revolutions," *Philosophical Review* 73, no. 3 (1964): 388.

2   Shapere, "The Structure," 390.

3   Shapere, "The Structure," 391.

4   The story of the confrontation between Kuhn and Popper is well captured in Steve Fuller, *Kuhn vs Popper: The Struggle for the Soul of Science* (New York: Columbia University Press, 2004).

5   Fuller, *Kuhn vs Popper*, 29.

6   Karl Popper, "Normal Science and Its Dangers," in *Criticism and the Growth of Knowledge*, ed. Imre Lakatos and A. Musgrave (Cambridge: Cambridge University Press, 1970), 55.

7   Paul Hoyningen-Huene, *Reconstructing Scientific Revolutions: Thomas S. Kuhn's Philosophy of Science* (Chicago, IL: University of Chicago Press, 1993), 168.

8   Popper, "Normal Science," 53.

9   James A. Marcum, Thomas Kuhn's *Revolution: An Historical Philosophy of Science* (London: Continuum, 2005), 86–7.

10 John Worrall, "Normal Science and Dogmatism, Paradigms and Progress: Kuhn 'Versus' Popper and Lakatos," in *Thomas Kuhn*, ed. Thomas Nickles (Cambridge: Cambridge University Press, 2003), 67–9.

11 J. Watkins, "'Against "Normal Science"'," in *Criticism and the Growth of Knowledge*, ed. Lakatos and Musgrave, 37.

12 Vasso Kindi and Theodore Arabatzis, "Introduction," in *Kuhn's The Structure of Scientific Revolutions Revisited*, ed. Vasso Kindi and Theodore Arabatzis (New York: Routledge, 2012), 2.

13 Marcum, *Thomas Kuhn's Revolution*, 87.

14 Imre Lakatos, "Falsification and the Methodology of Scientific Research Programmes," in *Criticism and the Growth of Knowledge*, ed. Lakatos and Musgrave, 93.

15 Marcum, *Thomas Kuhn's Revolution*, 101.

16 Thomas S. Kuhn, "Logic of Discovery or Psychology of Research?," in *Criticism and the Growth of Knowledge* ed. Lakatos and Musgrave, 20.

17 Kuhn, "Logic of Discovery," in *Criticism and the Growth of Knowledge*, ed. Lakatos and Musgrave 1.

18 Thomas S. Kuhn, "The Function of Dogma in Scientific Research," in *Scientific Change*, ed. Alistair C. Crombie (New York: Basic Books, 1963), 347–69.

19 Thomas Kuhn, "Second Thoughts on Paradigms," in *The Essential Tension: Selected Studies in Scientific Tradition and Change* (Chicago, IL: University of Chicago Press, 1977), 259, 295–319.

20 See Paul Hoyningen-Huene's detailed analysis of the components of the disciplinary matrix in *Reconstructing Scientific Revolutions*, 145–59.

21 Hoyningen-Huene, *Reconstructing Scientific Revolutions*, 143.

22 W.H. Newton-Smith, *The Rationality of Science* (London: Routledge, 1981), 12; Hilary Putnam, *Reason, Truth and History* (Cambridge: Cambridge University Press, 1981), 115.

23 Thomas S. Kuhn, "Postscript," *The Structure of Scientific Revolutions*, 4th ed. (Chicago, IL: University of Chicago Press, 2012), 197–203.

24 Howard Sankey, "Kuhn's Changing Concept of Incommensurability," *British Journal for the Philosophy of Science* 44, no. 4 (1993): 765.

25 Kuhn, "Postscript," *Structure*, 201–2.

26 Hoyningen-Huene, *Reconstructing Scientific Revolutions*, 219–21.

27 Thomas S. Kuhn, "Theory-Change as Structure-Change: Comments on the Sneed Formalism," *Erkenntnis* 10, no. 2 (1976): 191.

28 Newton-Smith, *The Rationality of Science*, 113–4; Putnam, *Reason, Truth and History,* 126; M.V. Curd, "Kuhn, Scientific Revolutions and the Copernican Revolution," *Nature and System* 6 (1984): 4.

29 Worrall, "Normal Science," 93.

30 Musgrave, "Kuhn's Second Thoughts," 293; Shapere, "The Paradigm Concept," Science 172 (1971): 707.

31 Shapere, "The Paradigm Concept," 708.

32 Shapere, "The Paradigm Concept," 710.

33 Peter Godfrey-Smith, *An Introduction to the Philosophy of Science: Theory and Reality* (Chicago, IL: University of Chicago Press, 2003), 87.

MODULE 10
THE EVOLVING DEBATE

KEY POINTS

- *The Structure of Scientific Revolutions* became a point of reference for sociologists of science and working scientists themselves as an ever-broadening array of scholars debated scientific concepts, often out of their context.

- Although no Kuhnian school of thought exists today, his work has had wide-ranging impact of history work in philosophy, history, sociology,* psychology, and in the natural sciences.

- Kuhn's work has given rise to a new debate within the sub-discipline of the sociology of scientific knowledge,* exploring how scientists' tastes affect their conclusions.

Uses and Problems

Thomas Kuhn's *The Structure of Scientific Revolutions* is regarded by scholars as a seminal work both for those studying the history of science,* for students of the sociology and philosophy of knowledge (and sociology more generally), and for those working in the educational and non-profit sectors to promote public engagement with science.

Like his contemporaries, the philosophers Paul Feyerabend,* Karl Popper* and Norwood Russell Hanson,* Kuhn presented radical reinterpretations of science that ended the domination of the logical-empiricist* school of thought. More than any of his contemporaries, "Kuhn changed the philosophy of science* by describing a tremendously vivid picture of scientific change."[1]

> **❝** The basic problem is that there are, as philosopher of science Tim Maudlin has eloquently pointed out, *two* Kuhns—a moderate Kuhn and his immoderate brother—jostling elbows throughout the pages of *The Structure of Scientific Revolutions.* **❞**
>
> Alan Sokal and Jean Bricmont, *Intellectual Impostures*

Although *Structure* generated considerable controversy when it was first published, it is difficult, perhaps, to detect the impact of the ideas and problems it offered in the work of subsequent scholars.

The philosopher of science Ian Hacking* argued in 1981 that *The Structure of Scientific Revolutions* put an end to several dominant concepts, the most notable being, arguably, that of realism*—the idea that science can discover truths about the real world.[2] Other scholars find that *Structure* has had a minimal impact on the philosophy of science. Hanne Andersen,* Peter Barker,* and Xiang Chen,* for example, philosophers of science from Denmark, Britain, and the US respectively, argue that philosophers of science have developed negative perceptions of Kuhn's work because of mistakes that have persisted for nearly a half century. They believe that contemporary philosophy of science has withdrawn from historical studies; instead, it concentrates on defending the realist position (that scientific facts can only be determined by observation) against the constructivist* position (that scientists determine facts by observing reality and interpreting it in accordance with their beliefs.)[3]

Schools of Thought

Kuhn's work falls between currents of thought in the history and philosophy of science and no strictly Kuhnian school of thought exists. Scholars agree that Kuhn's work proved highly provocative for historians of science, even if those historians adopted few of its propositions. The American historian of philosophy Jan Golinski,* for example, claims that Kuhn's "influence among historians has been at best limited"[4] (a view shared by the scholars Vasso Kindi* and Theodore Arabatzis*).[5]

These views have persisted despite the efforts of Kuhn's own students to spread his approach to the history of science. The American academic John L. Heilbron,* for example, wrote that Kuhn "gave us to understand that we were engaged in an intellectual adventure of great moment."[6] Historians of science—especially N. M. Swerdlow,* J. Z. Buchwald* and Norton Wise*—took up Kuhn's notions of the scientific community,* scientific revolutions* and incommensurability* to further his research agenda and the cyclical understanding of scientific progress.[7]

In the 1970s, the movement away from Kuhn's work gave rise to externalist* approaches to the way scientists conduct research. These approaches emphasized that science is the product of external factors such as society and political events, and paid less, if any, attention to the requirements of scientific accuracy and integrity.

In the 1990s, the field moved on to new concerns, for which Kuhn had no answers. Kuhn's critique of the older understandings of science ironically led to the discipline dismissing him as representative of the "outmoded genre of grand narratives."[8] In other words, historians chose to abandon internalist* assumptions such as those Kuhn highlighted when explaining how scientists chose the consensus paradigm,* turning instead to new methods, particularly from sociology, seeking to convey more than the "pallid* platitudes" about science seen from the inside.[9]

This movement has continued into the 1990s and early 2000s with the rising tide of externalist readings focused on the work of the influential French philosopher Michel Foucault,* who saw social determinants as paramount in the search for understanding.[10]

In Current Scholarship

Currently, radical intellectuals remain the most avid proponents of Thomas Kuhn's text. *The Structure of Scientific Revolutions* has become a foundational piece of writing for postmodernist* critiques of science, which question the possibility of objectivity in science, considering it a form of cultural production like any other and subject to the same issues of context and interpretation. These approaches have spurred new sub-genres of scholarship such as feminist* and post-colonial* studies. These new disciplines seek to demonstrate that, although ignored by previous scholars, women and colonial subjects had a place in the history of science.[11] As the science interpreter Ziauddin Sardar* points out, Kuhn has been considered to be "subversive of science" by those eager to preserve what little remains of the internalist reading of science presented by logical empiricists (meaning those trying to save scientists' claims to objectivity while simultaneously exploring how personal and professional factors shape scientific practice).[12]

Kuhn's ideas remain central to the sociology of scientific knowledge,[13] an approach formulated by the sociologists David Bloor* and Barry Barnes* of the University of Edinburgh which maintains that social conditions create scientific knowledge.[14] The French sociologist Bruno Latour* and his colleague Stephen Woolgar* produced the most infamous example of this approach. "Our most general objective," they wrote in the preface to *Laboratory Life* (1969), "is to shed light on the nature of 'the soft underbelly of science': we therefore focus on the work done by a scientist located firmly at his laboratory bench."[15] By "soft underbelly" they mean the malleable social conditions that, they allege, shape science.

Most recently, postmodernist critics of science have turned their focus to the role of science in society. As Sardar has observed, science is a field that exercises considerable power and authority, remaining deeply tied up with globalized* corporate and government capital. These newest critics center their debate on the importance and level of public scrutiny of science.

Radical critics of science argue that today science has become so closely linked with political and economic power structures—government and global corporations—that historians and philosophers of science, as neutral or disinterested observers, need to scrutinize scientists' activity in the same way that politicians' and lobbyists' motives and conflicts of interest are examined. Such critics have also questioned the billions Western countries spend on scientific research each year.[16]

Some still support a vision of science as independent and autonomous. These critics counter that the "academic Left" cannot properly understand what science is and how it works. Embedded in this is a criticism of the language of multiculturalism.* The mathematician and physicist Alan Sokal* has said that, in an environment that prizes multiculturalism, "incomprehensibility becomes a virtue; allusions, metaphors and puns substitute for evidence and logic."[17] He argues that postmodernist scholarship has resulted in the loss of public faith in science—a loss, as he sees it, hindering progress. As the biologist E. O. Wilson* succinctly (and sarcastically) put it in a 1994 talk, "multiculturalism equals relativism* equals no supercollider equals communism."*[18] In other words, Sokal and Wilson argue that once the credibility of scientific work comes into question, as it has since Kuhn and especially with the work of postmodernists, then it loses funding from government, corporations, and academic foundations. This means, ultimately, that scientific experiment will not continue and so the contribution of scientific work to public health and living standards will collapse, leaving the world in a state of ignorance. This, they contend, represents a step backwards that should not take place—no matter how imperfect the current state of science may be.

NOTES

1   Peter Godfrey-Smith, *An Introduction to the Philosophy of Science: Theory and Reality* (Chicago, IL: University of Chicago Press, 2003), 98.

2   Ian Hacking, *Scientific Revolutions* (Oxford: Oxford University Press, 1981), 1–2.

3   Hanne Andersen, Peter Barker and Xiang Chen, *The Cognitive Structure of Scientific Revolutions* (Cambridge: Cambridge University Press, 2006), 238.

4   Jan Golinski, *Making Natural Knowledge: Constructivism and the History of Science* (Cambridge: Cambridge University Press, 1998), 14.

5   Vasso Kindi and Theodore Arabatzis, "Introduction," in *Kuhn's The Structure of Scientific Revolutions Revisited*, ed. Vasso Kindi and Theodore Arabatzis (New York: Routledge, 2012), 2.

6   John L. Heilbron, "A Mathematicians' Mutiny, with Morals," in *World Changes: Thomas Kuhn and the Nature of Science*, ed. Paul Horwich (Cambridge, MA: MIT Press, 1993), 112.

7   James A. Marcum, *Thomas Kuhn's Revolution: An Historical Philosophy of Science* (London: Continuum, 2005),134–6.

8   Kindi and Arabatzis, "Introduction," 2.

9   Kindi and Arabatzis, "Introduction," 3.

10 Peter Novick, *The Noble Dream: The "Objectivity Question" and the American Historical Profession* (Cambridge: Cambridge University Press, 1988), 536–7.

11 Ziauddin Sardar, "Thomas Kuhn and the Science Wars," in *Postmodernism and Big Science*, ed. Richard Appignanesi (Cambridge: Icon Books, 2002), 216–21.

12 Sardar, "Thomas Kuhn and the Science Wars," 221.

13 Barry Barnes, *T.S. Kuhn and Social Science* (London: Macmillan, 1982).

14 David Bloor, *Knowledge and Social Imagery*, 2nd ed. (Chicago, IL: Chicago University Press, 1991), 7,166.

15 Bruno Latour and Steve Woolgar, *Laboratory Life: The Construction of Scientific Facts* (New York: Sage Publications, 1979), 27.

16 Sardar, "Thomas Kuhn and the Science Wars," 6.

17 Alan Sokal, "A Physicist Experiments with Cultural Studies," *Lingua Franca* (1996), 62–4.

18 Quoted in Michael Bérubé, "The Science Wars Redux," *Democracy Journal* 19 (2011): 67.

MODULE 11
IMPACT AND INFLUENCE TODAY

KEY POINTS

- *The Structure of Scientific Revolutions* presents a contested understanding of scientific knowledge that continues to stimulate debate and misunderstanding across the social sciences and philosophy today.

- Scholars situate Kuhn's work between the logical positivist* school (with its emphasis on formal methods) and the relativist* school (with its assumption that ultimate, "perfect" solutions to scientific questions are impossible). But it poses challenges to each.

- Responses to Kuhn's work continued into the twenty-first century as the rise of postmodernism* prompted scholars to increasingly contest the notion that science is useful for other subjects.

Position

In 1993 the German American philosopher of science Carl Hempel* anointed Thomas Kuhn's *The Structure of Scientific Revolutions* a landmark history of science.* Hempel opened a collection of essays about the philosophy of science* by addressing Kuhn directly: "Whatever position your colleagues may take, Tom, I am sure that they all feel a large debt of gratitude to you for your provocative and illuminating ideas."[1] Hempel's tribute is especially noteworthy because Kuhn's work challenged the logical–empiricist* approach taken by Hempel.

Many scholars find that the work had the least impact where Kuhn would have wanted it to have the most: on the history of science. In fact, recent critics allege "Kuhn's effect on science studies has been to dull the importance of history and paralyze the discussion of politics."[2]

" Fifty years ago this month, one of the most influential books of the twentieth century was published by the University of Chicago Press. Many if not most lay people have probably never heard of its author, Thomas Kuhn, or of his book, *The Structure of Scientific Revolutions*, but their thinking has almost certainly been influenced by his ideas. The litmus test is whether you've ever heard or used the term "paradigm shift," which is probably the most used—and abused—term in contemporary discussions of organisational change and intellectual progress. A Google search for it returns more than 10 million hits, for example. And it currently turns up inside no fewer than 18,300 of the books marketed by Amazon. It is also one of the most cited academic books of all time. So if ever a big idea went viral, this is it. "

John Naughton, "Thomas Kuhn: The Man Who Changed the Way the World Looked at Science"

Certainly the work, with its emphasis on history and culture, contributed to the demise of logical empiricism, a school founded on notions of objectivity and purely verifiable analysis. But its positive influence on the philosophy of science remains less clear. Although the unprecedented response to Kuhn's work has made it famous, it has also prevented *The Structure of Scientific Revolutions* from making a lasting and definable contribution to the subject Kuhn prized most: the history of science. In part, this must be because that response has focused more on the philosophical content of Kuhn's argument— concepts such as paradigm,* incommensurability* and exemplar*— rather than the historical reading of science on which Kuhn based these concepts.

Interaction

The Structure of Scientific Revolutions remains part of the current intellectual debate on science. But Kuhn might not be comfortable with the direction of the debate today in which the battle lines are drawn between science realists* (who believe, roughly, that we arrive at scientific facts through observation) and constructivists* (who consider science a matter of interpretation in which the scientist's beliefs play a significant part).

The debate between these two factions exploded in the 1990s in the so-called "science wars."* In this period realist supporters—mainly practitioners and some philosophers of science—attacked as "irrational" cultural and postmodernist ideas, frequently held by people on the political Left. The American scientists Paul Gross* and Norman Levitt* fired the first shot in this "war" in 1994 when they published *Higher Superstition*, a book in which they decried postmodernism as "medieval" in outlook and condemned the academic Left's bias against science.[3] They followed this with a 1995 conference in New York City called "The Flight from Science and Reason." Papers presented at the conference condemned criticism of science as "common nonsense" and critics as "charlatans."[4]

In the 2000s, Gross, Levitt, and some of those they attacked on the Left took steps to end the argument. But the quarrel persists because it has a bearing on how universities distribute funds for scientific research—money lying at the root of this "war," as it does in so many real-life conflicts. To Gross and Levitt, challenging the concrete conclusions of science undermines its credibility and marginalizes it in universities.[5] On the Left, the American philosopher Michael Bérubé* argues that what postmodernists really object to is "fundamentalism" about science being untouchable. By drawing the battle lines against this view, all parties may be able to unite since Gross, Levitt, and Bérubé all desire the practice of high-quality science that is open to debate. All of them share with Kuhn a desire to improve the role of science in society through a better understanding of how it works; all differ from Kuhn in that, by opening science to debate, they take away its status as untouchable (something that Kuhn guarded).

Nevertheless, the issue of science's position in society does not necessarily translate into clear-cut political stances. As Bérubé noted: "The 1990s have not been kind to American institutions of higher education. Academy bashing is now amongst the fastest-growing of major US industries."[6] University funding in general came under attack in the twenty-first century, and this has added an additional layer of logistical tension to the intellectual debates between scholars and scientists discussing the nature of scientific research.

The Continuing Debate

The Structure of Scientific Revolutions is now in its fourth edition. The latest, a 50th anniversary edition, prompted a renewed wave of interest in Kuhn's work.[7] *Structure* continues to provoke and compel those thinking about radical changes in the state of knowledge generally. Even when scholars work in fields far distant from Kuhn's history of science—in history, anthropology, and sociology, for example—they continue to speak in terms of the "structure of revolutions" and "paradigm shifts"* as Kuhn defined the term.[8]

Beyond the academic community, Kuhn himself retains a reputation as a radical opponent of entrenched norms of scientific and academic behavior. In fact, people sometimes see him as a proto-postmodernist—having begun the postmodern interest in including under-represented and marginalized groups in science. Because the reputation of *The Structure of Scientific Revolutions* has widened beyond scientific circles, several terms in the book have entered general use. These include the idea of scientific revolution as an upheaval in scientific knowledge and—most famously— the terms "paradigm" and "paradigm shift." We now hear these equally in popular culture and intellectual environments. Indeed, the expression "paradigm shift" became an Internet buzzword in the late 1990s. Promoters of online shopping used it to convince customers to change their shopping habits.[9] In 2001, *The Complete Idiot's Guide to a Smart Vocabulary* referred to "paradigm shift" as a phrase so overused that it has become meaningless.[10]

NOTES

1   Carl Hempel, "Thomas Kuhn: Colleague and Friend," in *World Changes: Thomas Kuhn and the Nature of Science*, ed. Paul Horwich (Cambridge, MA: MIT Press, 1993), 7–8.

2   Esther-Mirjam Sent, "Review of Steve Fuller, *Thomas Kuhn: A Philosophical History of our Times*," *The Review of Politics* 63, no. 2 (2001): 392.

3   Paul Gross and Norman Levitt, *Higher Superstition: The Academic Left and Its Quarrels with Science* (Baltimore, MA: Johns Hopkins University Press, 1994).

4   Ziauddin Sardar, "Thomas Kuhn and the Science Wars," in *Postmodernism and Big Science*, ed. Richard Appignanesi (Cambridge: Icon Books, 2002), 189.

5   Peter Godfrey-Smith, *An Introduction to the Philosophy of Science: Theory and Reality* (Chicago, IL: University of Chicago Press, 2003), 146.

6   Michael Bérubé and Cary Nelson, eds, *Higher Education Under Fire: Politics, Economics and the Crisis of the Humanities* (New York: Routledge, 1995), 1.

7   Thomas Nickles, "Introduction," in *Thomas Kuhn*, ed. Thomas Nickles (Cambridge: Cambridge University Press, 2003), 1–19.

8   Carolyn Merchant, "The Theoretical Structure of Ecological Revolutions," in *Out of the Woods*, ed. Char Miller and Hal Rothman (Pittsburgh, PA: Pittsburgh University Press, 2014), 18–27.

9   Kent German, "Top 10 Buzzwords," *CNET*, accessed August 17, 2013, http://www.cnet.com/1990–11136_1–6275610–1.html.

10 Paul McFedries, *The Complete Idiot's Guide to a Smart Vocabulary* (New York: Alpha, 2001), 142–3.

MODULE 12
WHERE NEXT?

KEY POINTS

- *The Structure of Scientific Revolutions* will continue to play a part in debates about how the field of science should respond to attacks on the credibility of its status as an impartial accumulation of knowledge.

- It appears likely that scholars will continue to debate the meaning of Kuhn's work and its significance to the history and philosophy of science.*

- *The Structure of Scientific Revolutions* presented a radical and original understanding of scientific knowledge and practice. It also transformed the public image of scientists and transformed the concept of "paradigm"* into a household term. The work has also inspired generations of scientists and other scholars to reflect on the status of scientific knowledge.

Potential

In the half century since its first publication in 1962, Thomas Kuhn's *The Structure of Scientific Revolutions* has become emblematic of a transformation in the history of science.* As Kuhn himself observed, his work has received credit for more than its share of the revolution in the history of science. This seems likely to continue, as many aspects of the book make it ripe for reinterpretation.[1]

The potential of Kuhn's work lies in its usefulness to the ongoing debate between two schools of contemporary sociology*: the sociology of scientific knowledge* (according to which social conditions create scientific knowledge), and constructivist* sociology (according to which scientists do not study reality directly, they

> **66** The purpose of the 'Science Wars' * issue was to answer the 'shrill tone of backlash' against feminist, multiculturalist, and social critics of science ... a backlash designed to intimidate anyone who dares to question the gender-laden assumptions of science, the capitalist foundations of scientific empiricism* and the destructive effects of science and technology on society and environment. **99**
>
> Ziauddin Sadar, *Thomas Kuhn and the Science Wars*

"construct" it from the results of their experiments)—and also to postmodernist* and multicultural* critiques of science. In addition, it continues to challenge the possibility of balancing internalist* readings of science with a view that considers the circumstances in which scientists work.

Kuhn did not intend to spark most of these developments. In fact, he had intended the work for a limited audience of scientists, historians, and philosophers of science. But as long as scholars continue the debate, Kuhn's critique of cumulative, linear, scientific development should remain influential.

We may see Kuhn's book as a source of new ideas that have branched out in ways that he could not have foreseen and may reasonably expect that these branches will continue to flourish and develop. But we may also wonder to what extent these branches will continue to identify themselves as part of Kuhn's legacy. This will also determine whether scholars and practitioners in these fields will go back to the original text in search of new ideas to develop.[2]

Future Directions

In the absence of a Kuhnian school of thought, those most likely to further the potential of *The Structure of Scientific Revolutions* are the same scholars who responded energetically to Kuhn in the run-up to the publication of the 50th anniversary edition of *The Structure of Scientific Revolutions* in 2012.

These include the American historian and sociologist Steve Fuller* who wrote *Thomas Kuhn: A Philosophical History for Our Time* (2000), a study formed around the central question "how radical were Kuhn's ideas?" His answer is a resounding "not very." *Thomas Kuhn* (2000) by the British philosopher of science Alexander Bird* studies Kuhn as refracted through the central ideas of *Structure*, considered both individually, in the case of "paradigm" and "incommensurability,"* and as a whole in the context of the study of the philosophy of science. The American science philosopher Thomas Nickles* took the opportunity to collect together the latest scholarship on Kuhn's life, times, and work in the edited volume of essays *Thomas Kuhn* (2003). In *Thomas Kuhn's "Linguistic Turn" and the Legacy of Logical Empiricism* (2008), the Italian historian of science Stefano Gattei* focused specifically on the relationship between Kuhn's work and the logical empiricism* it purported to attack.

Kuhn's The Structure of Scientific Revolutions Revisited (2012), a work edited by the Greek historians of science Vasso Kindi* and Theodore Arabatzis,* took stock of recent directions in research prompted by Kuhn's work. In particular, the essays they collected examine the function of concepts in scientific research, logical positivism,* the relationship of history to the philosophy of science, and the nature of progress in science.

As impressive as this list is, these scholars merely study Kuhn's ideas. They do not try to apply them. So Kuhn's work may well remain no more than a chapter of the history of ideas.* As Ian Hacking explained in the anniversary edition of *The Structure of Scientific Revolutions*, "just because *Structure* is a great book, it can be read in endless ways and put to endless uses."[3] Future ideas inspired by Kuhn's work will likely be as much of a surprise to scholarship as *Structure* was when it first appeared in 1962.

Summary

The Structure of Scientific Revolutions deserves to be read for three interconnected reasons:

First, the work transformed our understanding of the nature and characteristics of science. It did so using concepts that have entered everyday language. Perhaps the most widely known of these are the ideas of the paradigm and the paradigm shift.* These concepts, and others discussed in *Structure*, will likely continue to be heard in households and schools and seminar rooms across the world.

Second, Kuhn's work stimulated dramatic changes beyond the history of science, affecting thought in philosophy and a range of social sciences. His notion of scientific revolution has become synonymous with human endeavor and discovery on a grand scale in a way that improves mankind's ability to live and flourish in the world.

Third, the demanding conceptual apparatus Kuhn deploys in his work offers a lesson in critical thought that can help readers of any discipline develop their critical faculties. This is another way in which the work reaches beyond science: even professionals working in business or the knowledge industry can benefit from Kuhn's thinking. In that sense, Kuhn's work may be one of the most broadly useful books of the twentieth century. It seems likely to retain its usefulness as we progress through the twenty-first.

NOTES

1   Thomas S. Kuhn, *The Road Since Structure: Philosophical Essays, 1970–1993 with an Autobiographical Interview*, ed. James Conant and John Haugeland (Chicago, IL: Chicago University Press, 2000), 90–1.

2   Marnie Hughes-Warrington, "Thomas Samuel Kuhn," in *Fifty Key Thinkers in History* (London: Routledge, 2003), 191–2.

3   Ian Hacking, "Introductory Essay," in Thomas S. Kuhn, *The Structure of Scientific Revolutions*, 4th ed. (Chicago, IL: University of Chicago Press, 2012), VIII.

GLOSSARY

GLOSSARY OF TERMS

Analytic proposition: a statement that is true because of what it means, usually a widely accepted statement of fact: "crows are black," for example.

Analytic–synthetic distinction: a distinction used by philosophers to separate factual or inherently true statements (analytic propositions) from those rendered true by virtue of what they say about the world (synthetic propositions).

Anomalies: in the context of Kuhn's concept of paradigm, these are discrepancies between the explanation provided by the paradigm and the aspects of reality it purports to explain. Anomalies cast doubt on paradigms that can lead to periods of crisis science and scientific revolutions.

Classical mechanics: applied mathematics concerned with the motion and equilibrium of bodies and the action of forces. Branches of classical mechanics include kinematics, dynamics, and statics.

Cognitive science: the field of study concerned with analyzing how people acquire and use the information they receive through their senses of sight, hearing, taste, and touch.

Cognitive worldview: the way in which people view the world around them by using their abstract ideas to connect perceptions of reality they gather through their sense of sight, sound, smell, touch, and taste. For example, we know from sight and touch that we stand on the ground as do most objects; we know from the idea of gravity that this is because of gravity, which we cannot otherwise sense.

Cold War: a period of military tension between the United States and the Soviet Union that lasted from the end of World War II until 1991, when the Soviet Union collapsed.

Communism: a political system in which the government takes ownership of industry, commerce, and farming, and runs them for the common good of the people.

Consensus paradigm: the paradigm scientists choose from the competing alternatives during periods of crisis science, the choice creating a scientific revolution.

Constructivist: an adherent to the school of thought called constructivism in the philosophy of science.

Constructivism: holds that scientists do not study reality directly but construct their understanding of it from information they collect through experiments.

Crisis science: a period of uncertainty that begins when anomalies between reality and a paradigm cast doubt on the consensus paradigm. This period may result in a scientific revolution, when a new consensus paradigm is chosen, or reversion to normal science if anomalies can be explained away with minor amendments to the consensus paradigm.

Darwinian theory: a theory of the evolution of species, according to which animals and organisms evolve by inheriting from their parents traits in their minds and bodies that increase their chances of competing, surviving, and reproducing.

Disciplinary matrix: in Kuhn's work, a scientific community's symbolic generalizations, models, values, and problem solutions that they use in their field of specialization.

Empirical: derived from the study of observable evidence rather than from assumptions or theory.

Empiricism: the view that all knowledge derives from the experience we gain of reality through our senses (sight, sound, touch, smell, and taste). In science, empiricism therefore emphasizes the importance of accurate experiments in order to "see" reality.

Empiricist: an adherent of empiricism who, in the context of science, advocates accurate experimentation in order to "see" reality.

Esoteric: used to describe language, schools of thought or any system of understanding as difficult to understand for an audience or reader with no prior knowledge. In other words, suitable for an inner circle of those in the know.

Exemplar: a well-known solution to a scientific problem developed under the consensus paradigm during a period of normal science that becomes a model for all scientists working under that paradigm to emulate.

Externalist: an approach to understanding science as the product of factors external to the scientific community and scientific experiment, such as social factors, political events, and economic determinants.

Extraordinary science: the period in between crisis science and a scientific revolution when multiple paradigms compete to explain a number of anomalies that have become too great for the existing consensus paradigm to survive. It is out of the ordinary (or "extraordinary") because scientific activity is a state of chaos.

Feminist: an agenda in politics and scholarship that promotes the equal rights and freedom of women to take any role in life they choose, even those roles traditionally seen as belonging exclusively to the realm of men.

Gestalt psychology: a school of psychology holding that perceptions to the world are "Gestalts"—thoughts and impressions produced by the mind when it connects perceptions of the world (sights, sounds, language) using theoretical frameworks such as ideas to make sense of them. Gestalt psychology assumes that we build a worldview by mentally ordering our experience in such a way that some individual, new, experience has the capacity to radically alter our understanding of what is "real" altogether.

Gestalt switch: a moment, according to Gestalt psychology, when an individual's perceptions change from one Gestalt to another. After Gestalt switches, people see the world differently from the way they had before.

Globalization: the process by which corporations, economies, and nation states have opened their operations and borders to global interaction and communication in the past 30 years, creating new, mass markets.

Harvard University: a leading private American research university based in Cambridge, Massachusetts, and founded in 1636.

Hiroshima: a Japanese city in western Honshu, one of two cities on which the US Air Force dropped atomic bombs in 1945, near the end of World War II.

History of ideas: the sub-discipline of history committed to the study of how people form and change ideas of the world in which they live over time as a function of their social, cultural, economic, political, and religious lives.

History of science: the sub-discipline of history that focuses on explaining and understanding the development of scientific knowledge over time.

History of Science Society: the society promotes interest in the history of science and its social and cultural relations across the United States. The presidency of the History of Science Society is an elected administrative office whose candidates are chosen by their peers on merit.

Idealism: a philosophical school of thought that argues reality is a construction of the human mind rather than something outside ourselves that we can investigate directly.

Incommensurability: a characteristic of paradigms meaning that they cannot fully understand, or borrow, each other's language, concepts or methodology in any way. Scientists working in different fields, each field having its own paradigm, cannot therefore collaborate easily across paradigms just as scientists in the same field cannot use past paradigms once a new consensus paradigm overturns them.

Internalism: a position in the philosophy of science that explains science purely in terms of scientists' behaviors and the nature of scientific practice. Internalists do not take external context into account.

Irrationality: the process of thinking about and reaching conclusions concerning any subject without forming reasonable interpretations of the subject according to widely accepted standards of logic. Contrasts with rationalism.

Logical empiricism: a movement in the philosophy of science that flourished in the early twentieth century. Logical empiricists insisted that science should analyze parts of reality to understand the whole. It also held that all scientists' conclusions can be verified by having other scientists re-running their experiments.

Logical positivism: theories and doctrines of the Vienna Circle philosophers in the early 1930s. It proposes that metaphysical, irrational, and speculative questions are logically ill-founded. Instead, logical positivism aims at evolving formal methods—similar to those of the mathematical sciences—to verify empirical questions in the language of philosophy.

Manhattan Project: a research project that designed and manufactured the first nuclear weapons in the world between 1942 and 1946, led by America but with the support of Canada and the United Kingdom.

Massachusetts Institute of Technology (MIT): a private research university based in Cambridge, Massachusetts, founded in 1861, originally with an emphasis on engineering and subjects relating to the technological advancement of the American economy.

Multiculturalism: policies designed to encourage and nurture to coexistence of different cultures within one society.

Nagasaki: a Japanese city on the island of Kyushu, one of two cities on which the US Air Force dropped an atomic bomb in 1945, near the end of World War II.

Normal science: the period during which a consensus paradigm rules the work of scientists in their field, and scientists work to amend the paradigm as their experimentation progresses.

Normative: a statement that judges or measures according to an ideal standard or norm rather than according to actual reality.

Oil crisis of 1973: the rise in oil prices from $3 to $12 (US) as a result of an oil export embargo against America, following American intervention in a Middle Eastern war between Israel and a coalition of Arab states led by Egypt and Syria. The crisis led to dramatic and sustained increases in the cost of living in Western nations.

Pallid: any object or organism lacking depth or intensity of color.

Paradigm: in Kuhn's understanding of science, a concept agreed by scientists that solves a scientific problem and also guides future scientific research until a paradigm shift.

Paradigm shift: when a paradigm reaches a state of incommensurability, scientists agree a new paradigm. This means they shift their allegiance from the old paradigm to the new.

Philosophy of science: the branch of philosophy that seeks to explain the foundational principles by which scientists conduct their work.

Post-colonial studies: a sub-discipline of the humanities committed to revising anthropology, history, and sociology (and other disciplines) to include the perspective of the persons and groups previously subjected to colonial rule. Most often, this includes countries in Africa, Asia, South America and elsewhere colonized by European powers.

Postmodernism: a movement in the humanities and social sciences that took hold by the end of the 1980s. It urged scholars to explore the role that previously unrepresented groups—women, ethnic and religious minorities, and marginalized sexualities—had played in creating the past.

Pre-consensus science: the earliest phases of scientific activity when scientists from rival schools compete to interpret phenomena. This competition is resolved when scientists choose the first paradigm according to which they all work, and the first period of normal science ensues.

Princeton University: a leading private research university in Princeton, New Jersey, founded in 1746.

Quantum mechanics: the branch of physics that studies the motion and interaction of the smallest particles. Quantum mechanics deepens the findings of classical mechanics by focusing on a smaller scale in the physical world.

Quantum physics: a branch of physics studying the smallest level of objects in the physical universe: atoms and atomic particles.

Rationalism: the philosophical school of thought that attaches importance to the use of logic and reasoned thought to solve problems rather than relying on intuition or faith.

Realism: the school of thought in the philosophy of science that argues scientists can access and describe reality directly without their own opinions and practices affecting the truth of their conclusions.

Relativism: a school of thought in science which holds that scientists reach provisional conclusions rather than absolute definitive results that will never change when they conduct their research.

Revolutionary science: the period during which several paradigms compete to become the consensus paradigm of a community of scientists, the original paradigm having become doubtful after reality throws up anomalies that it cannot explain.

Science wars: a series of intellectual exchanges in the 1990s and early 2000s when scientific realists and postmodernist critics debated the nature of science.

Scientific community: all the scientists working in the world at any one time.

Scientific revolution: the process occurring from time to time that causes the development of scientific knowledge, usually following new discoveries. During a revolution, scientists discard an old paradigm, starting instead to work in accordance with a new one that better explains the reality they investigate.

Sociology: the study of the structure and history of human societies.

Sociology of science: the branch of sociology that examines how scientists' social, economic, and professional positions help shape the research topics and conclusions produced in the scientific community.

Sociology of scientific knowledge (SSK): a school of thought within the sociology of science that takes inspiration from Kuhn's work and argues for a constructivist interpretation of science.

Soviet Union: the Union of Soviet Socialist Republics that existed from 1922 until 1991. Its center of power was Russia, but it also encompassed many other states, including Ukraine and Georgia.

Synthetic proposition: a statement that is true because of the way in which it relates to the world rather than because it is a statement of fact—for example, "crows attack small birds." The statement is not true of crows in general, but is borne out by the observable behavior of a majority of crows.

Tacit knowledge: knowledge not easily transferred from one person to another by the simple act of writing or speaking, including assumptions often taken almost for granted.

Teleology: the study of a subject such as the history of science as leading inevitably to an end or final cause. Teleology often comes in for criticism for ignoring the chaotic journey of science to its current form owing to excessive focus on the destination rather than the journey.

Theoretical physics: the branch of physics that relies on theory, mathematics, and abstract reasoning in order to present possible explanations of the natural world that could not be tested in a laboratory due to the size or nature of the subject considered. For example, one could not perform laboratory tests on the nature of the universe.

Unit ideas: the basic ideas and perceptions of the world that make no sense on their own until joined together by the thinking mind into a worldview, as explained by Arthur O. Lovejoy. For example, the idea that "the sky is blue" joins together unit ideas including being able to see a sky, being able to distinguish blue from other colors, and knowing the words "sky" and "blue."

Verifiability theory of meaning: a theory asserting that the meaning and truth of statements or scientific conclusions lies in the ability of a scientist to re-create an experiment conducted by her colleague and still reach the same conclusions, so checking its truth. If different conclusions result from the same experiment then the scientist has shown her colleague's finding to be false.

Verificationist principle: the rule that the conclusions of scientific experiment must be replicable by third parties when they repeat the same experiment in order for them to be true.

University of California, Berkeley: the leading research university in the University of California system and a major public-research university with an international reputation for its teaching and research.

World War I (1914–18): the global armed conflict between the Allied powers (Britain, France, Russia, and the United States) on the one side and the Central Powers (Germany, the Ottoman Empire and Austria-Hungary) on the other.

World War II (1939–45): the global armed conflict between the Allied powers (Britain, France, Russia, and the United States) and the Axis powers of Germany, Italy, Japan, and their satellite states.

PEOPLE MENTIONED IN THE TEXT

Hanne Andersen is a Danish philosopher of science in the Faculty of Technology and Science, Department of Mathematics and Science Studies at Aarhus University. She has studied Kuhn's work extensively, and works to make the philosophy of science relevant to scientific education.

Theodore Arabatzis is an associate professor of philosophy and history of science at the University of Athens, Greece. He has recently published *Representing Electrons* (2006).

Francis Bacon (1561–1626) was an English philosopher, statesman, lawyer, and writer. His main works are *Novum Organum Scientiarum* (1620) and *New Atlantis* (1627).

Peter Barker is a British historian and philosopher of science who currently holds the appointment of professor of history of science at the University of Oklahoma.

Barry Barnes (b. 1943) is a British philosopher of science, currently professor of sociology at the University of Exeter. He worked with David Bloor from the 1970s to the 1990s at the University of Edinburgh to develop the strong program of the sociology of scientific knowledge.

George Berkeley (1685–1753) was a British philosopher and one of the principal exponents of the British empiricist philosophy, according to which knowledge derives from experience, not reason. His main work is *A Treatise on the Principles of Human Knowledge* (1710).

Michael Bérubé (b. 1961) is an American philosopher and Professor and Director of the Institute for the Arts and Humanities at Pennsylvania State University, USA. He has written *Higher Education Under Fire* (1995).

Alexander Bird is a British philosopher of science and professor of philosophy at the University of Bristol. He wrote *Thomas Kuhn* (2000) and *Philosophy of Science* (1998).

David Bloor (b. 1942) is a British sociologist and professor of science and technology studies at the University of Edinburgh. He is best known for having established the strong program of sociology of scientific knowledge, particularly in his work *Knowledge and Social Imagery* (1978).

J. Z. Buchwald (b. 1949) is an American historian of science who is currently Doris and Henry Dreyfuss Professor of History at the California Institute of Technology at Pasadena, California. He has written on a variety of history of science topics including an edited volume on the practice of physics, *Scientific Practice: Theories and Stories of Doing Physics* (1995).

Rudolf Carnap (1891–1970) was a German logical-empiricist philosopher of science. He emigrated to the United States in 1935 and his main work is *Philosophy and Logical Syntax* (1935).

Xiang Chen is an Asian American philosopher of science, currently professor of philosophy at the California Lutheran University. The main contribution on the subject is Andersen, Barker and Chen, *The Cognitive Structure of Scientific Revolutions* (2006).

James Bryant Conant (1893–1978) was an American chemist, president of Harvard University and the first US ambassador to West Germany.

Nicolaus Copernicus (1473–1543) was a Polish Renaissance mathematician and astronomer who formulated the current idea that the sun is at the center of the universe and so the earth rotates around it.

Arthur Danto (1924–2013) was an American art critic and philosopher who contributed to a number of fields, notably historical theory. He is most widely remembered as an art critic for *The Nation*, the USA's oldest weekly magazine.

Charles Darwin (1809–82) was an English naturalist who proposed that all species of life have descended from common ancestors, and that evolution resulted from natural selection, or the survival of the fittest.

Pierre Duhem (1861–1916) was a French historian and philosopher of science. His masterpiece is *The System of the World* (1913–16), in which he famously argued for the continuation between medieval and early modern science.

Paul Feyerabend (1924–94) was an Austrian-born émigré to the United States and iconoclast philosopher of science. His main work is *Against Method* (1975).

Michel Foucault (1926–84) was a French philosopher, historian, social theorist, philologist, and psychologist, one of the twentieth century's most famous thinkers. His main work is *The Archaeology of Knowledge* (1969).

Michael Friedman (b. 1947) is an American philosopher of science who teaches and researches at Stanford University. His book *Dynamics of Reason* (2001) developed and explored areas of Kuhn's concept of paradigm shifts that Kuhn himself left under-developed.

Steve Fuller (b. 1959) is an American philosopher and sociologist. His main works are *Kuhn vs Popper* (2003) and *Science vs Religion?* (2007).

Stefano Gattei is an Italian philosopher of science who is a member of the faculty at the Institute for Advanced Studies, Lucca, Italy. His doctoral dissertation studied Kuhn's work: *La Rivoluzione Incompiuta di Thomas Kuhn* ("Thomas Kuhn's Incomplete Revolution") (2007).

Jan Golinski (b. 1957) is an American philosopher of science and a professor of history and humanities at the University of New Hampshire. He is the author of *Making Natural Knowledge* (1998).

Paul Gross is an American biologist and author of *Higher Superstition* (1994) with Norman Levitt, as well as *Creationism's Trojan Horse: The Wedge of Intelligent Design* (2004).

Ian Hacking (b. 1936) is an influential Canadian historian and philosopher of science. His main work is *The Emergence of Probability* (1975).

Norwood Russell Hanson (1924–67) was an American philosopher of science. He is best-known for arguing that when scientists observe the world they impose a host of preconceived theories on what they see.

John L. Heilbron (b. 1934) is an American historian of science, and professor of history at the University of California at Berkeley. His main work is *Electricity in the 17th and 18th Centuries: A Study of Early Modern Physics* (1979).

Carl Hempel (1905–97) was a German American philosopher of science and famous logical empiricist. His main work is *Scientific Explanation* (1967).

Richard Hofstadter (1916–70) was an American historian of American history in the modern and contemporary era. His work ranged widely across the history of ideas and social history more generally.

Paul Hoyningen-Huene (b. 1946) is a German philosopher of science best known for his neo-Kantian interpretation of Thomas Kuhn. His main work is *Reconstructing Scientific Revolutions: Thomas S. Kuhn's Philosophy of Science* (1993).

David Hume (1711–76) was a British philosopher, one of the principal exponents of British empiricist philosophy, according to which knowledge derives from experience, not reason. His main writing is *A Treatise of Human Nature* (1739).

Immanuel Kant (1724–1804) was a German philosopher and one of the most important thinkers of the modern age. His major work is *The Critique of Pure Reason* (1781).

Johannes Kepler (1571–1630) was a German mathematician and astronomer who played an important role in revising scientists' understanding of the world in the seventeenth century. His theory of the arrangement of the planets that gives us our current model of the universe forms his main contribution.

Vasso Kindi is a Greek philosopher of science who is assistant professor of philosophy and history of science at the University of Athens, Greece. Her main work so far is *Kuhn & Wittgenstein: Philosophical Investigation of the Structure of Scientific Revolutions* (1995).

Alexandre Koyré (1892–1964) was a French Russian émigré to the USA, who developed outstanding analyses of seventeenth-century history of science and helped coin the term "scientific revolution" to describe the intellectual changes of the period. His main work is *From the Closed World to the Infinite Universe* (1957).

Imre Lakatos (1922–74) was a Hungarian philosopher of science and mathematician. His main work is *The Methodology of Scientific Research Programmes* (1978).

Bruno Latour (b. 1947) is a French sociologist of science and anthropology. His main works, *Science in Action* (1987) and *Laboratory Life* (1979), are famous for reducing scientists' work to the results of their social circumstances.

Antoine Lavoisier (1743–94) was a French chemist widely considered the "father of modern chemistry" and the leader of the "chemical revolution" of the late eighteenth century.

Norman Levitt (1943–2009) was an American mathematician at Rutgers University, USA. He is mainly remembered for his book *Higher Superstition* (1994), co-authored with Paul Gross.

John Locke (1632–1704) was an English philosopher considered a British empiricist and the father of classical liberalism. His main work is *An Essay of Human Understanding* (1690).

Arthur O. Lovejoy (1873–1962) was a German-born American émigré renowned for his book *The Great Chain of Being* (1936) that began the modern study of the history of ideas.*

Ernst Mach (1838–1916) was a German philosopher and author of *The Science of Mechanics* (1883), which emphasized empiricism over metaphysics.

Anneliese Maier (1905–71) was a German historian of science. A selection of her writings was published in English as *On the Threshold of Exact Science: Selected Writings of Anneliese Maier on Late Medieval Natural Philosophy* (1982).

James A. Marcum is an American philosopher of science who works at Baylor University, Waco, Texas. He has studied the development of science and written most recently *The Conceptual Foundations of Systems Biology: An Introduction* (2009).

Margaret Masterman (1910–86) was a British linguist and philosopher, best known for her pioneering studies of computational linguistics and automatic computer translation.

Hélène Metzger (1889–1944) was an influential French historian and philosopher of science. Her main works are *Les Doctrines Chimiques en France du Début du XVIIe à la Fin du XVIIIe siècle* ("The Doctrines of Chemistry in France from the Beginning of the Seventeenth until the End of the Eighteenth Century") (1923).

Alan Musgrave (b. 1940) is a New Zealand philosopher of science. He was a student of Karl Popper and author of *Common Sense, Science and Scepticism* (1992).

Otto Neurath (1882–1945) was an Austrian logical–positivist philosopher and leader of the Vienna Circle of philosophy of science. Neurath's main English-language book is *Empiricism and Sociology* (1973).

Isaac Newton (1642–1727) was an English physicist and mathematician whose work pioneered the laws of motion and the modern theory of gravity. He is best known for his *Principia Mathematica* ("Mathematical Principles") (1687).

Thomas Nickles is an American philosopher of science who is Foundation Professor at the University of Nevada, Reno. He has written widely on Kuhn as well as other areas of the history of science.

George Orwell (1903–50) is the pen name of Eric Arthur Blair, an English novelist and journalist. He is famous for his dystopian novel *Nineteen Eighty-Four* (1949) and his novella *Animal Farm* (1945), both of which condemned overbearing governments.

Jean Piaget (1896–1980) was a Swiss psychologist and philosopher who propounded a famous theory of cognitive development in children. His main works are *The Origins of Intelligence in Children* (1953) and The *Child's Construction of Reality* (1955).

Max Planck (1858–1947) was a German theoretical physicist who is deemed the founder of quantum theory, which won him the Nobel Prize in Physics in 1918.

Michael Polanyi (1891–1976) was a British Hungarian philosopher of science and a chemist. His most famous works are *Personal Knowledge* (1958) and *The Tacit Dimension* (1966).

Karl Popper (1902–94) was a British Austrian philosopher of science, widely considered one of the greatest of the twentieth century. His most famous work is *The Logic of Scientific Discovery* (1934).

Willard Van Orman Quine (1908–2000) was an influential American philosopher and logician. His main work is *Word and Object* (1960).

Jerry Ravetz (b. 1929) is an American philosopher of science and environment consultant who is best known for his work on the uncertainty and the ethics of scientific research. His book *A No-Nonsense Guide to Science* (2005) is his best-known contribution in this direction.

George A. Reisch is an American historian of science best known for his externalist studies of science, for example, *How the Cold War Transformed the Philosophy of Science* (2005).

Howard Sankey is an Australian philosopher of science who is currently associate professor of philosophy at the University of Melbourne. He is the author of *The Incommensurability Thesis* (1993).

Ziauddin Sardar (b. 1951) is a well-known British writer, scholar, and public figure. He has written numerous books, including *Reading the Qur'an* (2011) and *Thomas Kuhn and the Science Wars* (2000).

George Sarton (1884–1956) was a Belgian-born American chemist and historian of science. He intended to write a nine-volume history of science but at the time of his death had completed only three.

Dudley Shapere was an American philosopher of science and professor at Wake Forest University. He is mainly remembered for his harsh criticism of Thomas Kuhn and Paul Feyerabend.

Alan Sokal (b. 1955) is professor of mathematics at University College London and professor of physics at New York University.

N. M. Swerdlow (b. 1941) is professor emeritus of history, astronomy, and astrophysics at the University of Chicago, and visiting professor at the California Institute of Technology.

Harry S. Truman (1884–1972) was an American politician and 33rd president of the United States from 1945–53, the period immediately after World War II during which the Cold War began.

E. O. Wilson (b. 1929) is an American biologist, naturalist, and author, who is the world's leading expert on ants and a retired Harvard professor. His most recent work is *The Meaning of Human Existence* (2014).

Norton Wise (b. 1940) is Distinguished Professor of History at the University of California at Los Angeles. His research focuses on science and industrialization from the eighteenth century to the present.

Ludwig Wittgenstein (1889–1961) is often considered the greatest philosopher of the twentieth century; his main works are *Tractatus Logico-Philosophicus* (1921) and *Philosophical Investigations* (1953).

Stephen Woolgar (b. 1950) is a British sociologist, currently Head of Science and Technology Studies at the Said Business School, University of Oxford. He co-authored *Laboratory Life* (1979) with Bruno Latour.*

John Worrall (b. 1946) is professor of philosophy of science at the London School of Economics. He was a student of Imre Lakatos and is the author of *The Ontology of Science* (1994).

John M. Ziman (1925–2005) was a British-born physicist based in New Zealand whose work proved profession-leading in condensed-matter physics. His widest reputation outside science is as a spokesperson for science, and *Real Science* (2000) is his best-known publication on that topic.

WORKS CITED

WORKS CITED

Andersen, Hanne, Peter Barker and Xiang Chen. *The Cognitive Structure of Scientific Revolutions*. Cambridge: Cambridge University Press, 2006.

"Kuhn's Mature Philosophy of Science and Cognitive Psychology." *Philosophical Psychology* 9 (1996): 347–63.

Barker, Peter, Xiang Chen and Hanne Andersen. "Kuhn on Concepts and Categorization." In *Thomas Kuhn*, edited by Thomas Nickles, 212–45. Cambridge: Cambridge University Press, 2003.

Barnes, Barry. *T.S. Kuhn and Social Science*. London: Macmillan, 1982.

Bérubé, Michael. "The Science Wars Redux." *Democracy Journal* 19 (2011): 66–74.

Bérubé, Michael and Cary Nelson, eds. *Higher Education Under Fire: Politics, Economics and the Crisis of the Humanities.* New York: Routledge, 1995.

Bird, Alexander. "The Structure of Scientific Revolutions: An Essay Review of the Fiftieth Anniversary Edition." *The British Journal for the Philosophy of Science* 63, no. 4 (2012): 859–83.

Thomas Kuhn. Chesham: Acumen, 2000.

"Thomas Kuhn." *The Stanford Encyclopedia of Philosophy* (Winter 2014 Edition). Edited by Edward N. Zalta. Accessed July 8, 2015. http://plato.stanford.edu/archives/win2012/entries/davidson/>.

Bloor, David. *Knowledge and Social Imagery*. 2nd ed. Chicago, IL: University of Chicago Press, 1991.

Chang, Hasok. "Incommensurability: Revisiting the Chemical Revolution." In *Kuhn's The Structure of Scientific Revolutions Revisited*, edited by Vasso Kindi and Theodore Arabatzis, 153–79. New York: Routledge, 2012.

Curd, M.V. "Kuhn, Scientific Revolutions and the Copernican Revolution." *Nature and System* 6 (1984): 1–14.

Danto, Arthur. *Narration and Knowledge.* New York: Columbia University Press, 1985.

Feyerabend, Paul. "Consolations for the Specialist." In *Criticism and the Growth of Knowledge*, edited by Imre Lakatos and A. Musgrave, 197–229. Cambridge: Cambridge University Press, 1970.

Friedman, Michael. "Kuhn and Logical Empiricism." In *Thomas Kuhn*, edited by Thomas Nickles, 19–44. Cambridge: Cambridge University Press, 2003.

"Remarks on the History of Science and the History of Philosophy." In *World Changes: Thomas Kuhn and the Nature of Science*, edited by Paul Horwich, 37–54. Cambridge, MA: MIT Press, 1993.

Fuller, Steve. *Kuhn vs Popper: The Struggle for the Soul of Science*. New York: Columbia University Press, 2004.

Thomas Kuhn: A Philosophical History for Our Times. Chicago, IL: University of Chicago Press, 2000.

Gattei, Stefano. *Thomas Kuhn's "Linguistic Turn" and the Legacy of Logical Empiricism*. Burlington, VT: Ashgate, 2008.

German, Kent. "Top 10 Buzzwords," *CNET*. Accessed August 17, 2013. http:// The Structure of Scientific Revolutions.cnet.com/1990–11136_1–6275610–1. html.

Godfrey-Smith, Peter. *An Introduction to the Philosophy of Science: Theory and Reality*. Chicago, IL: University of Chicago Press, 2003.

Green, Christopher. "Where Is Kuhn Going?" *American Psychologist* 59, no. 4 (2004): 271–72.

Gross, Paul, and Norman Levitt. *Higher Superstition: The Academic Left and Its Quarrels with Science*. Baltimore, MD: Johns Hopkins University Press, 1994.

Hacking, Ian. "Introductory Essay." In Thomas Kuhn, *The Structure of Scientific Revolutions*, 4th edition, vii–xxxvii Chicago, IL: University of Chicago Press, 2012.

Scientific Revolutions. Oxford: Oxford University Press, 1981.

The Social Construction of What? Cambridge, MA: Harvard University Press, 1999.

Hall, A. Rupert. *The Revolution in Science 1500–1750*. London: Longman, 1983.

Hall, Marie Boas. "Review of *The Structure of Scientific Revolutions*." *American Historical Review* 68, no. 3 (1963): 700–1.

Heilbron, John L. "A Mathematicians' Mutiny, with Morals." In *World Changes: Thomas Kuhn and the Nature of Science*, edited by Paul Horwich, 81–129. Cambridge, MA: MIT Press, 1993.

"Thomas Samuel Kuhn." *Isis* 89, no. 3 (1998): 505–15.

Hempel, Carl. "Thomas Kuhn: Colleague and Friend." In *World Changes: Thomas Kuhn and the Nature of Science*, edited by Paul Horwich, 7–8. Cambridge, MA: MIT Press, 1993.

Hoftstadter, Richard. *Social Darwinism in American Thought, 1860–1915*. Boston, MA: Beacon, 1944.

Horwich, Paul. "Introduction." In *World Changes: Thomas Kuhn and the Nature of Science*, edited by Paul Horwich, 1–5. Cambridge, MA: MIT Press, 1993.

Hoyningen-Huene, Paul. *Reconstructing Scientific Revolutions: Thomas S. Kuhn's Philosophy of Science*. Chicago, IL: University of Chicago Press, 1993.

"Two Letters of Paul Feyerabend to Thomas S. Kuhn on a Draft of The Structure of Scientific Revolutions." *Studies in History and Philosophy of Science* 26, no. 3 (1995): 353–88.

Hughes, Jeff. "Whigs, Prigs and Politics: Problems in the Historiography of Contemporary Science." In *The Historiography of Contemporary Science and Technology*, edited by Thomas Söderqvist, 19–39. Amsterdam: Harwood Academic Publishers, 1997.

Hughes-Warrington, Marnie. *Fifty Key Thinkers on History*. London: Routledge, 2003.

Irzik, Gurol, and Teo Grünberg. "Carnap and Kuhn: Arch Enemies or Close Allies?" *British Journal for the Philosophy of Science* 46, no. 3 (1995): 285–307.

Jewett, Andrew. *Science, Democracy and the American University: From the Civil War to the Cold War*. Cambridge: University of Cambridge Press, 2012.

Kindi, Vasso, and Theodore Arabatzis, "Introduction." In *Kuhn's The Structure of Scientific Revolutions Revisited*, edited by Vasso Kindi and Theodore Arabatzis, 1–15. New York: Routledge, 2012.

Kuhn, Thomas S. "Afterwords." In *World Changes: Thomas Kuhn and the Nature of Science*, edited by Paul Horwich, 311–43. Cambridge, MA: MIT Press, 1993.

Black Body Theory and Quantum Discontinuity, 1894–1912. Chicago, IL: Chicago University Press, 1978.

"Concepts of Cause in the Development of Physics." In *The Essential Tension: Selected Studies in Scientific Tradition and Change*, 21–31. Chicago, IL: University of Chicago Press, 1977.

The Copernican Revolution: Planetary Astronomy in the Development of Western Thought. Cambridge, MA: Harvard University Press, 1957.

"The Function of Dogma in Scientific Research." In *Scientific Change,* edited by Alistair C. Crombie, 347–69. New York: Basic Books, 1963.

"The Function of Measurement in Modern Physical Sciences." In *The Essential Tension: Selected Studies in Scientific Tradition and Change*, 178–225. Chicago, IL: University of Chicago Press, 1977.

"Logic of Discovery or Psychology of Research?" In *Criticism and the Growth of Knowledge: Proceedings of the International Colloquium in the Philosophy of Science*, edited by Imre Lakatos and A. Musgrave, 1–23. Cambridge: Cambridge University Press, 1970.

"Objectivity, Value Judgement and Theory Choice." In *The Essential Tension: Selected Studies in Scientific Tradition and Change*, edited by Thomas S. Kuhn, 320–39. Chicago, IL: Chicago University Press, 1977.

"The Relations between the History and the Philosophy of Science," in *The Essential Tension: Selected Studies in Scientific Tradition and Change*, 1–21. Chicago, IL: University of Chicago Press, 1977.

The Road Since Structure: Philosophical Essays, 1970–1993 with an Autobiographical Interview. Edited by James Conant and John Haugeland. Chicago, IL: Chicago University Press, 2000.

"Second Thoughts on Paradigms." In *The Essential Tension: Selected Studies in Scientific Tradition and Change*, 295–319. Chicago, IL: University of Chicago Press, 1977.

The Structure of Scientific Revolutions, 4th edition. Chicago, IL: University of Chicago Press, 2012.

"Theory-Change as Structure-Change: Comments on the Sneed Formalism." *Erkenntnis* 10 (1976): 179–99.

Lakatos, Imre. "Falsification and the Methodology of Scientific Research Programmes." In *Criticism and the Growth of Knowledge*, edited by Imre Lakatos and A. Musgrave, 91–195. Cambridge: Cambridge University Press, 1970.

Latour, Bruno and Steve Woolgar. *Laboratory Life: The Construction of Scientific Facts.* New York: Sage Publications, 1979.

Longino, Helen E. "Does the Structure *of Scientific Revolutions* Permit a Feminist Revolution in Science?" In *Thomas Kuhn*, edited by Thomas Nickles, 261–81. Cambridge: Cambridge University Press, 2003.

Mandelbaum, Maurice. "A Note on Thomas S. Kuhn's *The Structure of Scientific Revolutions.*" *The Monist* 60, no. 4 (1977): 445–52.

Marcum, James A. *Thomas Kuhn's Revolution: An Historical Philosophy of Science*. London: Continuum, 2005.

Margolis, Joseph. "Objectivity as a Problem." *Annals of the American Academy of Political and Social Science* 560 (1998): 55–68.

Martin, R. N. D. *Pierre Duhem: Philosophy and History in the Work of a Believing Physicist*. La Salle, IL: Open Court, 1991.

Massimi, Michela. "Philosophy and the Sciences After Kant." In *Conceptions of Philosophy,* edited by Anthony O'Hear, 275–312. Cambridge: Cambridge University Press, 2000.

Masterman, Margaret. "The Nature of a Paradigm." In *Criticism and the Growth of Knowledge*, edited by Imre Lakatos and A. Musgrave, 59–89. Cambridge: Cambridge University Press, 1970.

McFedries, Paul. *The Complete Idiot's Guide to a Smart Vocabulary*. New York: Alpha, 2001.

Merchant, Carolyn. "The Theoretical Structure of Ecological Revolutions." In *Out of the Woods*, edited by Char Miller and Hal Rothman, 18–27. Pittsburgh, PA: Pittsburgh University Press, 2014.

Musgrave, Alan. "Kuhn's Second Thoughts." *British Journal for the Philosophy of Science* 22, no. 3 (1971): 287–97.

Nersessian, Nancy. "Kuhn, Conceptual Change, and Cognitive Science." In *Thomas Kuhn*, edited by Thomas Nickles, 178–211. Cambridge: Cambridge University Press, 2003.

Naughton, John. "Thomas Kuhn: The Man Who Changed the Way the World Looked at Science." *Guardian*, August 19, 2012. Accessed July 10, 2015. http://www.theguardian.com/science/2012/aug/19/thomas-kuhn-structure-scientific-revolutions.

Newton-Smith, W. H. *The Rationality of Science*. London: Routledge, 1981.

Nickles, Thomas. "Introduction." In *Thomas Kuhn*, edited by Thomas Nickles, 1–19. Cambridge: Cambridge University Press, 2003.

Novick, Peter. *That Noble Dream: The "Objectivity Question" and the American Historical Profession*. Cambridge: Cambridge University Press, 1988.

Popper, Karl. "Normal Science and Its Dangers." In *Criticism and the Growth of Knowledge*, edited by Imre Lakatos and A. Musgrave, 51–8. Cambridge: Cambridge University Press, 1970.

Putnam, Hilary. *Reason, Truth and History*. Cambridge: Cambridge University Press, 1981.

Reeves, Thomas C. *Twentieth-Century America: A Brief History*. Oxford: Oxford University Press, 2000.

Reisch, George A. "Did Kuhn Kill Logical Empiricism?" *Philosophy of Science* 58 (1991): 264–77.

Rouse, Joseph. "Kuhn's Philosophy of Scientific Practice." In *Thomas Kuhn*, edited by Thomas Nickles, 100–21. Cambridge: Cambridge University Press, 2003.

Sankey, Howard. "Kuhn's Changing Concept of Incommensurability." *British Journal for the Philosophy of Science* 44, no. 4 (1993): 759–74.

Sardar, Ziauddin. "Thomas Kuhn and the Science Wars." In *Postmodernism and Big Science*, edited by Richard Appignanesi, 189–228. Cambridge: Icon Books, 2002.

Sarkar, Sahotra. *The Legacy of the Vienna Circle: Modern Reappraisals*. New York: Garland Publishing, 1996.

Sarton, George. *A Guide to the History of Science*. Waltham, MA: Chronica Botanica Co, 1952.

Sent, Esther-Mirjam. "Review of Steve Fuller, *Thomas Kuhn: A Philosophical History of our Times*." *The Review of Politics* 63, no. 2 (2001): 390–2.

Shapere, Dudley. "The Paradigm Concept." *Science* 172 (1971): 706–9.

"The Structure of Scientific Revolutions." *Philosophical Review* 73, no. 3 (1964): 383–94.

Sokal, Alan. "A Physicist Experiments with Cultural Studies." *Lingua Franca* (1996): 62–4.

Swerdlow, N. M. "Thomas S. Kuhn, A Biographical Memoir." *National Academy of Science* (2013). Accessed June 29, 2015, http://www.nasonline.org/publications/biographical-memoirs/memoir-pdfs/kuhn-thomas.pdf.

"Science and Humanism in the Renaissance: Regiomontanus's Oration on the Dignity and Unity of the Mathematical Sciences." In *World Changes: Thomas Kuhn and the Nature of Science*, edited by Paul Horwich, 131–68. Cambridge, MA: MIT Press, 1993.

Watkins, J. "Against 'Normal Science.'" In *Criticism and the Growth of Knowledge*, edited by Imre Lakatos and A. Musgrave, 25–37. Cambridge: Cambridge University Press, 1970.

Wise, Norton M. "Mediations: Enlightenment Balancing Acts, or the Technologies of Rationalism." In *World Changes: Thomas Kuhn and the Nature of Science*, edited by Paul Horwich, 207–56. Cambridge, MA: MIT Press, 1993.

Wittgenstein, Ludwig. *Philosophical Investigations*, 3rd ed. Oxford: Blackwell, 2003.

Worrall, John. "Normal Science and Dogmatism, Paradigms and Progress: Kuhn 'Versus' Popper and Lakatos." In *Thomas Kuhn*, edited by Thomas Nickles, 65–100. Cambridge: Cambridge University Press, 2003.

Ziman, John M. *Real Science: What It Is and What it Means*. Cambridge: Cambridge University Press, 2000.

THE MACAT LIBRARY
BY DISCIPLINE

AFRICANA STUDIES

Chinua Achebe's *An Image of Africa: Racism in Conrad's Heart of Darkness*
W. E. B. Du Bois's *The Souls of Black Folk*
Zora Neale Huston's *Characteristics of Negro Expression*
Martin Luther King Jr's *Why We Can't Wait*
Toni Morrison's *Playing in the Dark: Whiteness in the American Literary Imagination*

ANTHROPOLOGY

Arjun Appadurai's *Modernity at Large: Cultural Dimensions of Globalisation*
Philippe Ariès's *Centuries of Childhood*
Franz Boas's *Race, Language and Culture*
Kim Chan & Renée Mauborgne's *Blue Ocean Strategy*
Jared Diamond's *Guns, Germs & Steel: the Fate of Human Societies*
Jared Diamond's *Collapse: How Societies Choose to Fail or Survive*
E. E. Evans-Pritchard's *Witchcraft, Oracles and Magic Among the Azande*
James Ferguson's *The Anti-Politics Machine*
Clifford Geertz's *The Interpretation of Cultures*
David Graeber's *Debt: the First 5000 Years*
Karen Ho's *Liquidated: An Ethnography of Wall Street*
Geert Hofstede's *Culture's Consequences: Comparing Values, Behaviors, Institutes and Organizations across Nations*
Claude Lévi-Strauss's *Structural Anthropology*
Jay Macleod's *Ain't No Makin' It: Aspirations and Attainment in a Low-Income Neighborhood*
Saba Mahmood's *The Politics of Piety: The Islamic Revival and the Feminist Subject*
Marcel Mauss's *The Gift*

BUSINESS

Jean Lave & Etienne Wenger's *Situated Learning*
Theodore Levitt's *Marketing Myopia*
Burton G. Malkiel's *A Random Walk Down Wall Street*
Douglas McGregor's *The Human Side of Enterprise*
Michael Porter's *Competitive Strategy: Creating and Sustaining Superior Performance*
John Kotter's *Leading Change*
C. K. Prahalad & Gary Hamel's *The Core Competence of the Corporation*

CRIMINOLOGY

Michelle Alexander's *The New Jim Crow: Mass Incarceration in the Age of Colorblindness*
Michael R. Gottfredson & Travis Hirschi's *A General Theory of Crime*
Richard Herrnstein & Charles A. Murray's *The Bell Curve: Intelligence and Class Structure in American Life*
Elizabeth Loftus's *Eyewitness Testimony*
Jay Macleod's *Ain't No Makin' It: Aspirations and Attainment in a Low-Income Neighborhood*
Philip Zimbardo's *The Lucifer Effect*

ECONOMICS

Janet Abu-Lughod's *Before European Hegemony*
Ha-Joon Chang's *Kicking Away the Ladder*
David Brion Davis's *The Problem of Slavery in the Age of Revolution*
Milton Friedman's *The Role of Monetary Policy*
Milton Friedman's *Capitalism and Freedom*
David Graeber's *Debt: the First 5000 Years*
Friedrich Hayek's *The Road to Serfdom*
Karen Ho's *Liquidated: An Ethnography of Wall Street*

John Maynard Keynes's *The General Theory of Employment, Interest and Money*
Charles P. Kindleberger's *Manias, Panics and Crashes*
Robert Lucas's *Why Doesn't Capital Flow from Rich to Poor Countries?*
Burton G. Malkiel's *A Random Walk Down Wall Street*
Thomas Robert Malthus's *An Essay on the Principle of Population*
Karl Marx's *Capital*
Thomas Piketty's *Capital in the Twenty-First Century*
Amartya Sen's *Development as Freedom*
Adam Smith's *The Wealth of Nations*
Nassim Nicholas Taleb's *The Black Swan: The Impact of the Highly Improbable*
Amos Tversky's & Daniel Kahneman's *Judgment under Uncertainty: Heuristics and Biases*
Mahbub Ul Haq's *Reflections on Human Development*
Max Weber's *The Protestant Ethic and the Spirit of Capitalism*

FEMINISM AND GENDER STUDIES

Judith Butler's *Gender Trouble*
Simone De Beauvoir's *The Second Sex*
Michel Foucault's *History of Sexuality*
Betty Friedan's *The Feminine Mystique*
Saba Mahmood's *The Politics of Piety: The Islamic Revival and the Feminist Subject*
Joan Wallach Scott's *Gender and the Politics of History*
Mary Wollstonecraft's *A Vindication of the Rights of Woman*
Virginia Woolf's *A Room of One's Own*

GEOGRAPHY

The Brundtland Report's *Our Common Future*
Rachel Carson's *Silent Spring*
Charles Darwin's *On the Origin of Species*
James Ferguson's *The Anti-Politics Machine*
Jane Jacobs's *The Death and Life of Great American Cities*
James Lovelock's *Gaia: A New Look at Life on Earth*
Amartya Sen's *Development as Freedom*
Mathis Wackernagel & William Rees's *Our Ecological Footprint*

HISTORY

Janet Abu-Lughod's *Before European Hegemony*
Benedict Anderson's *Imagined Communities*
Bernard Bailyn's *The Ideological Origins of the American Revolution*
Hanna Batatu's *The Old Social Classes And The Revolutionary Movements Of Iraq*
Christopher Browning's *Ordinary Men: Reserve Police Batallion 101 and the Final Solution in Poland*
Edmund Burke's *Reflections on the Revolution in France*
William Cronon's *Nature's Metropolis: Chicago And The Great West*
Alfred W. Crosby's *The Columbian Exchange*
Hamid Dabashi's *Iran: A People Interrupted*
David Brion Davis's *The Problem of Slavery in the Age of Revolution*
Nathalie Zemon Davis's *The Return of Martin Guerre*
Jared Diamond's *Guns, Germs & Steel: the Fate of Human Societies*
Frank Dikotter's *Mao's Great Famine*
John W Dower's *War Without Mercy: Race And Power In The Pacific War*
W. E. B. Du Bois's *The Souls of Black Folk*
Richard J. Evans's *In Defence of History*
Lucien Febvre's *The Problem of Unbelief in the 16th Century*
Sheila Fitzpatrick's *Everyday Stalinism*

The Macat Library By Discipline

Eric Foner's *Reconstruction: America's Unfinished Revolution, 1863-1877*
Michel Foucault's *Discipline and Punish*
Michel Foucault's *History of Sexuality*
Francis Fukuyama's *The End of History and the Last Man*
John Lewis Gaddis's *We Now Know: Rethinking Cold War History*
Ernest Gellner's *Nations and Nationalism*
Eugene Genovese's *Roll, Jordan, Roll: The World the Slaves Made*
Carlo Ginzburg's *The Night Battles*
Daniel Goldhagen's *Hitler's Willing Executioners*
Jack Goldstone's *Revolution and Rebellion in the Early Modern World*
Antonio Gramsci's *The Prison Notebooks*
Alexander Hamilton, John Jay & James Madison's *The Federalist Papers*
Christopher Hill's *The World Turned Upside Down*
Carole Hillenbrand's *The Crusades: Islamic Perspectives*
Thomas Hobbes's *Leviathan*
Eric Hobsbawm's *The Age Of Revolution*
John A. Hobson's *Imperialism: A Study*
Albert Hourani's *History of the Arab Peoples*
Samuel P. Huntington's *The Clash of Civilizations and the Remaking of World Order*
C. L. R. James's *The Black Jacobins*
Tony Judt's *Postwar: A History of Europe Since 1945*
Ernst Kantorowicz's *The King's Two Bodies: A Study in Medieval Political Theology*
Paul Kennedy's *The Rise and Fall of the Great Powers*
Ian Kershaw's *The "Hitler Myth": Image and Reality in the Third Reich*
John Maynard Keynes's *The General Theory of Employment, Interest and Money*
Charles P. Kindleberger's *Manias, Panics and Crashes*
Martin Luther King Jr's *Why We Can't Wait*
Henry Kissinger's *World Order: Reflections on the Character of Nations and the Course of History*
Thomas Kuhn's *The Structure of Scientific Revolutions*
Georges Lefebvre's *The Coming of the French Revolution*
John Locke's *Two Treatises of Government*
Niccolò Machiavelli's *The Prince*
Thomas Robert Malthus's *An Essay on the Principle of Population*
Mahmood Mamdani's *Citizen and Subject: Contemporary Africa And The Legacy Of Late Colonialism*
Karl Marx's *Capital*
Stanley Milgram's *Obedience to Authority*
John Stuart Mill's *On Liberty*
Thomas Paine's *Common Sense*
Thomas Paine's *Rights of Man*
Geoffrey Parker's *Global Crisis: War, Climate Change and Catastrophe in the Seventeenth Century*
Jonathan Riley-Smith's *The First Crusade and the Idea of Crusading*
Jean-Jacques Rousseau's *The Social Contract*
Joan Wallach Scott's *Gender and the Politics of History*
Theda Skocpol's *States and Social Revolutions*
Adam Smith's *The Wealth of Nations*
Timothy Snyder's *Bloodlands: Europe Between Hitler and Stalin*
Sun Tzu's *The Art of War*
Keith Thomas's *Religion and the Decline of Magic*
Thucydides's *The History of the Peloponnesian War*
Frederick Jackson Turner's *The Significance of the Frontier in American History*
Odd Arne Westad's *The Global Cold War: Third World Interventions And The Making Of Our Times*

LITERATURE

Chinua Achebe's *An Image of Africa: Racism in Conrad's Heart of Darkness*
Roland Barthes's *Mythologies*
Homi K. Bhabha's *The Location of Culture*
Judith Butler's *Gender Trouble*
Simone De Beauvoir's *The Second Sex*
Ferdinand De Saussure's *Course in General Linguistics*
T. S. Eliot's *The Sacred Wood: Essays on Poetry and Criticism*
Zora Neale Huston's *Characteristics of Negro Expression*
Toni Morrison's *Playing in the Dark: Whiteness in the American Literary Imagination*
Edward Said's *Orientalism*
Gayatri Chakravorty Spivak's *Can the Subaltern Speak?*
Mary Wollstonecraft's *A Vindication of the Rights of Women*
Virginia Woolf's *A Room of One's Own*

PHILOSOPHY

Elizabeth Anscombe's *Modern Moral Philosophy*
Hannah Arendt's *The Human Condition*
Aristotle's *Metaphysics*
Aristotle's *Nicomachean Ethics*
Edmund Gettier's *Is Justified True Belief Knowledge?*
Georg Wilhelm Friedrich Hegel's *Phenomenology of Spirit*
David Hume's *Dialogues Concerning Natural Religion*
David Hume's *The Enquiry for Human Understanding*
Immanuel Kant's *Religion within the Boundaries of Mere Reason*
Immanuel Kant's *Critique of Pure Reason*
Søren Kierkegaard's *The Sickness Unto Death*
Søren Kierkegaard's *Fear and Trembling*
C. S. Lewis's *The Abolition of Man*
Alasdair MacIntyre's *After Virtue*
Marcus Aurelius's *Meditations*
Friedrich Nietzsche's *On the Genealogy of Morality*
Friedrich Nietzsche's *Beyond Good and Evil*
Plato's *Republic*
Plato's *Symposium*
Jean-Jacques Rousseau's *The Social Contract*
Gilbert Ryle's *The Concept of Mind*
Baruch Spinoza's *Ethics*
Sun Tzu's *The Art of War*
Ludwig Wittgenstein's *Philosophical Investigations*

POLITICS

Benedict Anderson's *Imagined Communities*
Aristotle's *Politics*
Bernard Bailyn's *The Ideological Origins of the American Revolution*
Edmund Burke's *Reflections on the Revolution in France*
John C. Calhoun's *A Disquisition on Government*
Ha-Joon Chang's *Kicking Away the Ladder*
Hamid Dabashi's *Iran: A People Interrupted*
Hamid Dabashi's *Theology of Discontent: The Ideological Foundation of the Islamic Revolution in Iran*
Robert Dahl's *Democracy and its Critics*
Robert Dahl's *Who Governs?*
David Brion Davis's *The Problem of Slavery in the Age of Revolution*

The Macat Library By Discipline

Alexis De Tocqueville's *Democracy in America*
James Ferguson's *The Anti-Politics Machine*
Frank Dikotter's *Mao's Great Famine*
Sheila Fitzpatrick's *Everyday Stalinism*
Eric Foner's *Reconstruction: America's Unfinished Revolution, 1863-1877*
Milton Friedman's *Capitalism and Freedom*
Francis Fukuyama's *The End of History and the Last Man*
John Lewis Gaddis's *We Now Know: Rethinking Cold War History*
Ernest Gellner's *Nations and Nationalism*
David Graeber's *Debt: the First 5000 Years*
Antonio Gramsci's *The Prison Notebooks*
Alexander Hamilton, John Jay & James Madison's *The Federalist Papers*
Friedrich Hayek's *The Road to Serfdom*
Christopher Hill's *The World Turned Upside Down*
Thomas Hobbes's *Leviathan*
John A. Hobson's *Imperialism: A Study*
Samuel P. Huntington's *The Clash of Civilizations and the Remaking of World Order*
Tony Judt's *Postwar: A History of Europe Since 1945*
David C. Kang's *China Rising: Peace, Power and Order in East Asia*
Paul Kennedy's *The Rise and Fall of Great Powers*
Robert Keohane's *After Hegemony*
Martin Luther King Jr.'s *Why We Can't Wait*
Henry Kissinger's *World Order: Reflections on the Character of Nations and the Course of History*
John Locke's *Two Treatises of Government*
Niccolò Machiavelli's *The Prince*
Thomas Robert Malthus's *An Essay on the Principle of Population*
Mahmood Mamdani's *Citizen and Subject: Contemporary Africa And The Legacy Of Late Colonialism*
Karl Marx's *Capital*
John Stuart Mill's *On Liberty*
John Stuart Mill's *Utilitarianism*
Hans Morgenthau's *Politics Among Nations*
Thomas Paine's *Common Sense*
Thomas Paine's *Rights of Man*
Thomas Piketty's *Capital in the Twenty-First Century*
Robert D. Putman's *Bowling Alone*
John Rawls's *Theory of Justice*
Jean-Jacques Rousseau's *The Social Contract*
Theda Skocpol's *States and Social Revolutions*
Adam Smith's *The Wealth of Nations*
Sun Tzu's *The Art of War*
Henry David Thoreau's *Civil Disobedience*
Thucydides's *The History of the Peloponnesian War*
Kenneth Waltz's *Theory of International Politics*
Max Weber's *Politics as a Vocation*
Odd Arne Westad's *The Global Cold War: Third World Interventions And The Making Of Our Times*

POSTCOLONIAL STUDIES

Roland Barthes's *Mythologies*
Frantz Fanon's *Black Skin, White Masks*
Homi K. Bhabha's *The Location of Culture*
Gustavo Gutiérrez's *A Theology of Liberation*
Edward Said's *Orientalism*
Gayatri Chakravorty Spivak's *Can the Subaltern Speak?*

PSYCHOLOGY

Gordon Allport's *The Nature of Prejudice*
Alan Baddeley & Graham Hitch's *Aggression: A Social Learning Analysis*
Albert Bandura's *Aggression: A Social Learning Analysis*
Leon Festinger's *A Theory of Cognitive Dissonance*
Sigmund Freud's *The Interpretation of Dreams*
Betty Friedan's *The Feminine Mystique*
Michael R. Gottfredson & Travis Hirschi's *A General Theory of Crime*
Eric Hoffer's *The True Believer: Thoughts on the Nature of Mass Movements*
William James's *Principles of Psychology*
Elizabeth Loftus's *Eyewitness Testimony*
A. H. Maslow's *A Theory of Human Motivation*
Stanley Milgram's *Obedience to Authority*
Steven Pinker's *The Better Angels of Our Nature*
Oliver Sacks's *The Man Who Mistook His Wife For a Hat*
Richard Thaler & Cass Sunstein's *Nudge: Improving Decisions About Health, Wealth and Happiness*
Amos Tversky's *Judgment under Uncertainty: Heuristics and Biases*
Philip Zimbardo's *The Lucifer Effect*

SCIENCE

Rachel Carson's *Silent Spring*
William Cronon's *Nature's Metropolis: Chicago And The Great West*
Alfred W. Crosby's *The Columbian Exchange*
Charles Darwin's *On the Origin of Species*
Richard Dawkin's *The Selfish Gene*
Thomas Kuhn's *The Structure of Scientific Revolutions*
Geoffrey Parker's *Global Crisis: War, Climate Change and Catastrophe in the Seventeenth Century*
Mathis Wackernagel & William Rees's *Our Ecological Footprint*

SOCIOLOGY

Michelle Alexander's *The New Jim Crow: Mass Incarceration in the Age of Colorblindness*
Gordon Allport's *The Nature of Prejudice*
Albert Bandura's *Aggression: A Social Learning Analysis*
Hanna Batatu's *The Old Social Classes And The Revolutionary Movements Of Iraq*
Ha-Joon Chang's *Kicking Away the Ladder*
W. E. B. Du Bois's *The Souls of Black Folk*
Émile Durkheim's *On Suicide*
Frantz Fanon's *Black Skin, White Masks*
Frantz Fanon's *The Wretched of the Earth*
Eric Foner's *Reconstruction: America's Unfinished Revolution, 1863-1877*
Eugene Genovese's *Roll, Jordan, Roll: The World the Slaves Made*
Jack Goldstone's *Revolution and Rebellion in the Early Modern World*
Antonio Gramsci's *The Prison Notebooks*
Richard Herrnstein & Charles A Murray's *The Bell Curve: Intelligence and Class Structure in American Life*
Eric Hoffer's *The True Believer: Thoughts on the Nature of Mass Movements*
Jane Jacobs's *The Death and Life of Great American Cities*
Robert Lucas's *Why Doesn't Capital Flow from Rich to Poor Countries?*
Jay Macleod's *Ain't No Makin' It: Aspirations and Attainment in a Low Income Neighborhood*
Elaine May's *Homeward Bound: American Families in the Cold War Era*
Douglas McGregor's *The Human Side of Enterprise*
C. Wright Mills's *The Sociological Imagination*

Thomas Piketty's *Capital in the Twenty-First Century*
Robert D. Putman's *Bowling Alone*
David Riesman's *The Lonely Crowd: A Study of the Changing American Character*
Edward Said's *Orientalism*
Joan Wallach Scott's *Gender and the Politics of History*
Theda Skocpol's *States and Social Revolutions*
Max Weber's *The Protestant Ethic and the Spirit of Capitalism*

THEOLOGY

Augustine's *Confessions*
Benedict's *Rule of St Benedict*
Gustavo Gutiérrez's *A Theology of Liberation*
Carole Hillenbrand's *The Crusades: Islamic Perspectives*
David Hume's *Dialogues Concerning Natural Religion*
Immanuel Kant's *Religion within the Boundaries of Mere Reason*
Ernst Kantorowicz's *The King's Two Bodies: A Study in Medieval Political Theology*
Søren Kierkegaard's *The Sickness Unto Death*
C. S. Lewis's *The Abolition of Man*
Saba Mahmood's *The Politics of Piety: The Islamic Revival and the Feminist Subject*
Baruch Spinoza's *Ethics*
Keith Thomas's *Religion and the Decline of Magic*

COMING SOON

Chris Argyris's *The Individual and the Organisation*
Seyla Benhabib's *The Rights of Others*
Walter Benjamin's *The Work Of Art in the Age of Mechanical Reproduction*
John Berger's *Ways of Seeing*
Pierre Bourdieu's *Outline of a Theory of Practice*
Mary Douglas's *Purity and Danger*
Roland Dworkin's *Taking Rights Seriously*
James G. March's *Exploration and Exploitation in Organisational Learning*
Ikujiro Nonaka's *A Dynamic Theory of Organizational Knowledge Creation*
Griselda Pollock's *Vision and Difference*
Amartya Sen's *Inequality Re-Examined*
Susan Sontag's *On Photography*
Yasser Tabbaa's *The Transformation of Islamic Art*
Ludwig von Mises's *Theory of Money and Credit*

Printed in the United States
by Baker & Taylor Publisher Services